THE HOLY SPIRIT

A Bibliography

THE HOLY SPIRIT

A Bibliography

by Watson E. Mills

HENDRICKSON PUBLISHERS
PEABODY, MASSACHUSETTS 01961-3473

P.O. Box 3473
Peabody, Massachusetts 01961-3473

Printed in the United States of America.

ISBN 0913573-91-4

TABLE OF CONTENTS

PREFACE

More than twenty years ago I embarked on a study of glossolalia. The ensuing years have seen that interest continue and expand to the more general area of charismatic religion and the nature and work of the Holy Spirit.

In attempting to assemble a bibliography on a "live" field of study one is always aware of the limitations imposed by the enormity of the field and by the fact that there is often a lag between submission and publication. But despite these, and the obvious limitations of time and place, I offer what I hope will be at least a beginning point in bibliography on this very important subject.

The purpose here is to bring together in a single list the major works that have shaped the study of the Holy Spirit in the hope that this effort will itself not only produce a record of what has come before, but also that it may facilitate further research and clarification of this dimension of the faith.

I wish to express my sincere appreciation to Ms. Irene Palmer who worked tirelessly on the several drafts of these materials. Also, I express deep appreciation to President R. Kirby Godsey who has always generously supported my research efforts both financially and personally.

Watson E. Mills
Macon, Georgia
November 1987

ABBREVIATIONS

AA *American Anthropologist*
ABR *Australian Biblical Review*
ACQ *American Church Quarterly*
AER *African Ecclesiastical Review*
AJT *American Journal of Theology*
AM *American Mercury*
ARSSR *Annual Review of the Social Sciences of Religions*
ASSR *Archives de Sciences Sociales des Religions*
ATJ *African Theological Journal*
ATR *Anglican Theological Review*
ATRSS *Anglican Theological Review Supplement Series*
AV *Angelicum Vita*
AveM *Ave Maria*
AZQR *AME Zion Quarterly Review*
BBFL *Blue Banner Faith and Life*
BBHS *Baptists and the Baptism of the Holy Spirit*
BETS *Bulletin of the Evangelical Theological Society*
BHH *Baptist History and Heritage*
BI *Biblical Illustrator*
Bib *Biblica*
BibTr *Bible Translator*
BibZ *Biblische Zeitschrift*
BL *Bibel und Leben*
BLT *Brethren Life and Thought*
BQ *Baptist Quarterly*
BR *Biblical Review*
BRQ *Biblical Research Quarterly*
BRR *Baptist Reformation Review*
BS *Bibliotheca Sacra*
BTB *Biblical Theology Bulletin*
C *Catholisisme*
Cat *Catholica*
CBQ *Catholic Biblical Quarterly*

CH *Christian Herald*
Chm *Churchman*
ChrCent *Christian Century*
ChrCris *Christianity and Crisis*
ChSoc *Christian Society*
CL *Christianity and Literature*
CN *Coniectanea Neotestamentica*
Col *Collage*
Com *Communio (U.S.)*
Common *Commonweal*
Con *Contacts*
Conc *Consensus*
Concil *Concilium*
ConJ *Concordia Journal*
CQ *Covenant Quarterly*
CQR *Church Quarterly Review*
CS *Chicago Studies*
CSR *Christian Scholar's Review*
CT *Christianity Today*
CTJ *Calvin Theological Journal*
CTM *Currents in Theology and Mission*
CTQ *Concordia Theological Quarterly*
CV *Commmunio Viatorum*
DG *Drew Gateway*
Dia *Dialog*
Diak *Diakonia*
DL *Doctrine and Life*
DR *Downside Review*
DV *Divinitas Veritas*
EB *Estudios biblicos*
EC *Evangelical Christian*
EChR *Eastern Churches Review*
EcR *Ecumenical Review*
EgTh *Eglise et Théologie*
EJ *Eranos Jahrbuch*
Enc *Encounter*
EP *Ekklesiastikos Pharos*
EQ *Evangelical Quarterly*
EsTe *Estudios Teol*

ETL *Ephemerides Theologicae Lovanienses*
ETR *Etudes théologiques et religieuses*
Ev *Evangelica*
EvTh *Evangelische Theologie*
ExT *Expository Times*
FH *Fides et Historia*
Flam *Flambeau*
Found *Foundations*
Ful *Fuldaer*
FV *Foi et Vie*
GOTR *Greek Orthodox Theological Review*
Greg *Gregorianum*
HJ *The Heythrop Journal*
HL *Home Life*
Hok *Hokchma*
HTR *Harvard Theological Review*
IJT *Indian Journal of Theology*
IKZ *Internationale Katholische Zeitschrift*
Int *Interpretation*
IntRMiss *International Review of Missions*
IR *Iliff Review*
Iren *Irenikon: Revue des Monies de Chevetogne*
IrTQ *Irish Theological Quarterly*
Istina *Istina*
JAAR *Journal of the American Academy of Religion*
JBL *Journal of Biblical Literature*
JCM *Journal of Church Music*
JCQ *Japanese Christian Quarterly*
JD *Journal of Dharma*
JES *Journal of Ecumenical Studies*
JETS *Journal of the Evangelical Theological Society*
JPC *Journal of Pastoral Care*
JPH *Journal of Presbyterian History*
JPTh *Journal of Psychology and Theology*
JR *Journal of Religion*
JRH *Journal of Religious History*
JSNT *Journal for the Study of the New Testament*
JSSR *Journal for the Scientific Study of Religion*
JTS *Journal of Theological Studies*

JTSA *Journal of Theology for Southern Africa*
KD *Kerygma and Dogma*
KTR *King's Theological Review*
LJ *Logos Journal*
LQ *Lutheran Quarterly*
LS *Lebendige Seelsorge*
LTQ *Lexington Theological Quarterly*
LV *Lumière et Vie*
LW *Lutheran World*
M *Missiology*
MC *Modern Churchman*
MM *Moody Monthly*
MSt *Mid-Stream*
MTSB *Moravian Theological Seminary Bulletin*
NT *Novum Testamentum*
NTS *New Testament Studies*
NTTid *Nederlands theologisch tijdschrift*
NZST *Neue Zeitschrift für Systematische Theologie und Religionsphilosophie*
O *Orientierung*
OC *One in Christ*
OCP *Orientalia Christiana Periodica*
OF *Orate Fratres*
OS *Ostkirchliche Studien*
P *Pneuma, Journal of the Society for Pentecostal Studies*
Para *Paraclete*
PE *Pentecostal Evangel*
PJ *Perkins Journal*
PL *Presbyterian Life*
PMV *Pro Mundi Vita*
Prot *Protestantesimo*
PRS *Perspectives in Religious Studies*
PRZ *Patristic and Byzantine Review*
PSB *Princeton Seminary Bulletin*
PsySp *Psychonomic Speech*
QR *Quarterly Review*
RBib *Revue Biblique*
RE *Review and Expositor*
RefJ *Reformed Journal*
RefR *Reformed Review*

RefThR *Reformed Theological Review*
RefW *Reformed World*
RelEd *Religious Education*
RelSt *Religious Studies*
ReSR *Recherches de Science Religieuse*
ReT *Redemption Tidings*
RevRel *Review for Religious*
RHistE *Revue d'Historie Ecclésiastique*
RHPR *Revue d'historie et de philosophie religieuses*
RHR *Revue de l'Historie des Religions*
RL *Religion in Life*
RQ *Reformation Quarterly*
RQu *Revue de Qumran*
RS *Religion and Society*
RSciRel *Recherches de science religieuse*
RSPT *Revue des Sciences Philosophiques et Théologiques*
S *Spiritus*
SA *Sociological Anaylsis*
SAM *South Africana Marburgensia*
SCJ *Sixteenth Century Journal*
SEAJT *South East Asia Journal of Theology*
SEs *Science et Esprit*
SJT *Scottish Journal of Theology*
SL *Studia Liturgica*
SLJ *Saint Luke Journal*
SMR *Saint Mark Review*
Sob *Sobornost*
Soj *Sojourners*
Sp *Spirit*
SQ *Shane Quarterly*
StMiss *Studia Missionalia*
SvTK *Svensk Teologisk Kvartalskrift*
SVTQ *Saint Vladimir's Theological Quarterly*
SWJT *Southwestern Journal of Theology*
T *Time*
TB *Tyndale Bulletin*
TD *Theology Digest*
TH *Thomist*
ThEv *Theologia Evangelica*

ThLit *Theologische Literaturzeitung*
ThSt *Theological Studies*
ThTo *Theology Today*
ThZ *Theologische Zeitschrift*
TJ *Trinity Journal*
Tra *Traditio*
TSFB *Theological Students Fellowship Bulletin*
UC *Unité chrétienne*
ULC *Urban Life and Culture*
USQR *Union Seminary Quarterly Review*
UT *Ultimate Reality*
UUC *Unitarian Universalist Christian*
VigChr *Vigiliae christianae*
Vo *Voice*
Wit *Witness*
WO *World Order*
Wor *Worship*
WTJ *Wesley Theological Journal*
WW *Word & World: Theology for Christian Ministry*
ZKG *Zeitschrift für Kirchengeschichte*
ZMR *Zeitschriften für Missionwissenschaft und Religionswissenschaft*
ZNW *Zeitschriften für die Neutestamentliche Wissenschaft*
ZRGG *Zeitschrift für Religions- und Geistgeschichte*
ZTK *Zeitschriften Theologie und Kirche*

A

0001 Abel, Troy D. *Better Felt Than Said: The Holiness Pentecostal Movement.* Markham Press, 1982.

0002 Aberle, David. "A Note on Relative Deprivation Theory as Applied to Millenarian and Other Cultic Movements," in *Reader in Comparative Religion,* William A. Lessa and Evon Z. Vogt, editors. 2nd ed. Harper and Row, 1965. Pp. 45–56.

0003 Abreu, Dylton Francioni de. "A Critical Study of Karl Barth's Concept of the Holy Spirit with a Special Emphasis on the 'Church Dogmatics.'" Unpublished dissertation, New Orleans Baptist Seminary, 1974.

0004 Adai, Jacob. *Der Heilige Geist als Gegenwart Gottes.* P. Lang, 1985.

0005 Adams, Moody P. *Jesus Never Spoke in Tongues.* Privately published, 1974.

0006 Adams, William S. "Liturgical Art: A Pastoral Perspective," *SLJ* 21 (Spring 1978): 289–302.

0007 Adkins, Leon McKinley. "An Awareness of the Holy Spirit." Unpublished dissertation, Drew University, 1978.

0008 Adler, Gerhard. *Die Jesus-Bewegung. Aufbruch der enttäuschten Jugend.* Patmos Verlag, 1972.

0009 Ageneau, Robert. "Le mouvement Pentecôte catholique," *S* 13 (1972): 211–15.

0010 Aghiorgoussis, Maximos. "Holy Eucharist in Ecumenical Dialogue: An Orthodox View," *JES* 13 (Spring 1976): 204–12.

0011 Agnew, Milton S. "Baptized with the Spirit," *WTJ* 14 (Fall 1979): 7–14.

0012 Agrimson, J. Elmo. "The Congregation and the Gifts," in *The Gifts of the Spirit and the Body of Christ,* Elmo J. Agrimson, editor. Augsburg Publishing Co., 1974. Pp. 99–112.

0013 Agrimson, J. Elmo, ed. *Gifts of the Spirit and the Body of Christ: Perspectives on the Charismatic Movement.* Augsburg Publishing Co., 1974.

0014 Ahern, Barnabas Mary. "The Law of the Spirit of Holiness," in *The Spirit of God in Christian Life,* Edward Malatesta, editor. Paulist Press, 1977. Pp. 3–22.

0015 Ahrens, Theodor. "Concepts of Power in a Melanesian and Biblical Perspective," *M* 5 (April 1977): 141–73.

0016 Aikman, Duncan. "The Holy Rollers," *AM* 15 (October 1928): 180–91.

0017 Ainslie, Peter. *Cultivating the Fruit of the Spirit.* Bethany Press, 1968.

0018 Albrecht, Barbara. *Kirche und Glaubenserfahrung.* Kyrios-Verlag, 1971.

0019 Aldwinckle, Russell F. *The Holy Spirit in the Church.* N.p., n.d.

0020 Alexander, Wilber. "The Spirit and the Written Word," in *The Stature of Christ,* Vern Carner and Gary Stanhiser, editors. Privately published, 1970. Pp. 167–95.

0021 Alland, Alexander. "Possession in a Revivalistic Negro Church," *JSSR* 1 (1962): 204–13.

0022 Allen, Charles L. *The Miracle of the Holy Spirit.* Revell Co., 1974.

0023 Allen, Jimmy. "The Corinthian Glossolalia: The Historical Setting, An Exegetical Examination, and a Contemporary Restatement." Unpublished dissertation, Southern Baptist Seminary, 1967.

0024 Allen, Ronald. *Pentecost and the World.* Oxford University Press, 1917.

0025 Allen, Stuart. *Tongue-Speaking Today: A Mark of Spirituality or Deception?* Berean Publishing Trust, 1971.

0026 von Allmen, Jean Jacques. "Prédicateur, Témoin de l'evangile," *Iren* 49:3 (1976): 333–49.

0027 Alphanderéry, Paul. "La glossolalie dans le prophétisme médiéval latin," *RHR* 104 (November 1931): 417–36.

0028 Alphin, Ruffin A. "1 Corinthians 12:13a—a Pauline Spirit Baptism." Unpublished thesis, Grace Seminary, 1984.

0029 Althaus, Paul. *Communio Sanctorum. Die Gemeinde im lutherischen Kirchengendanken.* Kaiser Verlag, 1929.

0030 Altmann, Eckhard. *Die Predigt als Kontaktgeschehen.* Calwer Verlag, 1963.

0031 Altrichter, M. "Katholische Pfingstbewegung," *O* 36:6 (1972): 70–72.

0032 Alvarez de Linera, A. "El glosolali y su interprete," *EB* 9 (1950): 193–208.

0033 Amoit, F. "Glossolalia," *C* 5 (1962): 67–69.

0034 Amstutz, John. "Beyond Pentecost: A Study of Some Sociological Dimensions of New Testament Church Growth from the Book of Acts," in *Essays on Apostolic Themes: Studies in Honor of Howard M. Ervin,* Paul Elbert, editor. Hendrickson Publishers, 1985. Pp. 208–25.

0035 Anderson, E. Howard. *Receive the Holy Spirit.* Privately published, n.d.

0036 Anderson, Gerald H. and Thomas F. Stransky. *Faith Meets Faith.* Paulist Press, 1981.

0037 Anderson, Ray. "Notations on a Theology of the Holy Spirit: A Review Article," *TSFB* 4:5 (April 1981): 2–4.

0038 Anderson, Robert Mapes. "A Study of the Theology of the Episcopalians, the Lutherans, and the Pentecostals on the Charismata of the Holy Spirit." Unpublished dissertation, Concordia Theological Seminary, 1964.

0039 ______. *Vision of the Disinherited: The Making of American Pentecostalism.* Oxford University Press, 1979.

0040 Andrews, Edward D. *The People Called Shakers.* Oxford University Press, 1953.

0041 Andrews, Elias. "Ecstasy," in *Interpreter's Dictionary of the Bible,* George Arthur Buttrick, editor. 4 vols. Abingdon Press, 1962. A-D: 21–22.

0042 ______. "Spiritual Gifts," in *Interpreter's Dictionary of the Bible,* George Arthur Buttrick, editor. 4 vols. Abingdon Press, 1962. R-Z: 435–36.

0043 ______. "Tongues, Gift of," in *Interpreter's Dictionary of the Bible,* George Arthur Buttrick, editor. 4 vols. Abingdon Press, 1962. R-Z: 671–72.

0044 Andronikof, Constanin. "Y a-t-il une pneumatologie dans les fêtes fixes de la liturgie byzantine?" in *Le Saint-Esprit dans la Lit-*

urgie, A. Pistoia and A. Triacca, editors. Bibliotheca Ephemerides Liturgicae, 1977. Pp. 13–27.

0045 Anson, Gunars. "The Charismatics and Their Churches: Report on Two Conferences," *Dia* 15:2 (1976): 142–44.

0046 Antekeler, Charles. *Confirmation: The Power of the Spirit.* Ave Maria Press, 1972.

0047 Appia, Georges. "Une nouvelle Pentecôte," *UC* 28 (1972): 53–56.

0048 Arai, S. "Die Gegner des Paulus im 1 Korintherbrief und das Problem der Gnosis," *NTS* 19 (1972–73): 430–37.

0049 Aranda, A. *Estudios de Pneumatología.* Universidad de Navarra, 1985.

0050 van der Arendt, Gerrit. "Confirmation and Charismatic Renewal," *AER* 20 (October 1978): 276–81.

0051 Arichea, Daniel C., Jr. "The Holy Spirit and the Ordained Ministry," in *The Holy Spirit,* Dow Kirkpatrick, editor. Tidings, 1974. Pp. 158–86.

0052 Armstrong, Richard S. "The Integrity of Evangelism," *PSB* 3:2 (1981): 147–56.

0053 Arnal, Jean. *La Notion de l'esprit.* Librarie Fischbacher, 1907.

0054 Arnett, William M. "The Role of the Holy Spirit in Entire Sanctification in the Writings of John Wesley," *WTJ* 14 (Fall 1979): 15–30.

0055 Arnold, Eberhard. *Light and Fire and the Holy Spirit.* Plough Publishing Co., 1975.

0056 Arnot, Arthur B. "The Modern 'Speaking with Tongues,' " *EC* 46 (January 1950): 23–25, 59.

0057 Arrington, French L. "The Indwelling, Baptism, and Infilling with the Holy Spirit: A Differentiation of Terms," *P* 3:2 (Fall 1981): 1–10.

0058 Arsgène-Henry, Yolande d'Ormesson, ed. *Veni Sancte Spiritus.* Rüaber Verlag, 1959.

0059 Arthur, William. *The Tongues of Fire.* William Mullan & Son, 1877.

0060 Ashbrook, James B. "Praying for the Spirit," *RL* 46 (Spring 1977): 62–71.

0061 Ashcraft, Morris. "Glossolalia in the First Epistle to the Corinthians," in *Tongues,* Luther B. Dyer, editor. LeRoi Publishers, 1971. Pp. 60–84.

0062 ______. "Speaking in Tongues in the Book of Acts," in *Tongues,* Luther B. Dyer, editor. LeRoi Publishers, 1971. Pp. 85–104.

0063 Asociación de Iglesias Bautistas de Puerto Rica. *Lo que creemos los Bautistas: la doctrina del Espíritu Santo.* Rico Evangelico, 1935.

0064 Augsburger, Fred E. "Led by the Spirit," in *Encounter with the Holy Spirit,* George R. Brunk, II, editor. Herald Press, 1972. Pp. 63–80.

0065 Augsburger, Myron S. "The Holy Spirit and Evangelism," in *Encounter with the Holy Spirit,* George R. Brunk, II, editor. Herald Press, 1972. Pp. 231–42.

0066 ______. *Practicing the Presence of the Spirit.* Herald Press, 1982.

0067 ______. *Quench Not the Spirit.* Herald Press, 1962.

0068 Ausmus, Harry J. "Neitzsche and Eschatology," *JR* 58 (October 1978): 347–64.

0069 Autry, Arden Conrad. "Christ and the Spirit in the New Testament and in Christian Thought of the Second Century: A Comparative Study in Pneumatology." Unpublished dissertation, Baylor University, 1983.

0070 Axup, Edward J. *The Truth about Bible Tongues.* Privately published, 1933.

0071 Aykara, Thomas. "Feminine Aspect of God," *JD* 5 (April-June 1980): 127–211.

B

0072 Bach, Marcus. *The Inner Ecstasy.* Abingdon Press, 1969.

0073 ______. "Whether There Be 'Tongues,' " *CH* 87 (May 1964): 10–11, 20, 22.

0074 Baden, Hans Jürgen. *Es wird Zeit an Gott zu denken.* Agentur des Rauhen Hauses, 1970.

0075 Von Baer, Heinrich. *Der Heilige Geist in den Lukasschriften.* Kohlhammer, 1926.

0076 Baer, Richard A. "Quaker Silence, Catholic Liturgy, and Pentecostal Glossolalia—Some Functional Similarities," in *Perspectives on the New Pentecostalism,* Russell P. Spittler, editor. Baker Book House, 1976. Pp. 150–64.

0077 Baëta, C. G. *Prophetism in Ghana: A Study of Some "Spiritual" Churches.* SCM Press, 1962.

0078 Baillie, John. *Our Knowledge of God.* Oxford University Press, 1939.

0079 ______. *The Sense of the Presence of God.* Oxford University Press, 1962.

0080 Baird, John Stockton. "Preaching on the Holy Spirit in the Light of the New Testament Witness and the Preaching-Example of Selected Men." Unpublished dissertation, Temple University, 1960.

0081 Baker, J. B. "A Theological Look at the Charismatic Movement," *Chm* 86 (Winter 1972): 259–77.

0082 Baker, John. *Baptized in One Spirit: The Meaning of 1 Corinthians.* Fountain Trust, 1967.

0083 Baker, Kenneth Ward. "Father, Son and Holy Spirit in the Acts of the Apostles." Unpublished dissertation, Marquette University, 1967.

0084 Bales, Milton. *Types of the Holy Spirit.* Alliance Press, Co., n.d.

0085 Ball, Charles R. *The Dispensation of the Spirit.* SPCK, 1887.

0086 Ballenger, A. F. *Power for Witnessing.* Bethany Fellowship, Inc., 1963.

0087 Bammel, Ernst. "Jesus und der Paraklet in Johannes 16," in *Christ and Spirit in the New Testament: Essays in Honour of Charles Francis Digby Moule,* Barnabas Lindars, et al., editors. Cambridge University Press, 1973. Pp. 199–210.

0088 Banawiratma, Johannes. "Der Heilige Geist in der Theologie von Heribert Mühlen." Unpublished dissertation, University of Innsbruck, 1981.

0089 *The Baptism with the Holy Ghost and Fire.* Gospel Publishing House, n.d.

0090 Barbour, R. S. "Gethsemane in the Tradition of the Passion," *NTS* 16 (1969–70): 231–51.

0091 Barclay, William. *Flesh and Spirit.* SCM Press, 1962.

0092 ______. *The Promise of the Spirit.* Epworth, 1960.

0093 Barnard, A. C. "The Holy Spirit and Liturgy/Public Worship," in *The Spirit in Biblical Perspective,* W. S. Vorster, editor. University of South Africa, 1980. Pp. 48–63.

0094 Barnett, Maurice. *The Living Flame.* Epworth, 1953.

0095 Barrett, C. K. *The Holy Spirit and the Gospel Tradition.* SPCK, 1947.

0096 ______. "The Holy Spirit in the Fourth Gospel," *JTS* 1 (1950): 1–15.

0097 Barry, Joseph G. H. *Meditations on the Office and Work of the Holy Spirit.* The Young Churchman Co., 1922.

0098 Barth, Karl. *The Holy Ghost and the Christian Life.* Frederich Muller, 1938.

0099 Barth, Karl and Eduard Thurneysen. *Come Holy Spirit.* Mowbrays, 1977.

0100 Barth, Karl and Heinrich Barth. *Zur Lehre vom Heiligen Geist.* Raifer Verlag, 1930.

0101 Bartholomew, Clayton S. "Calvin's Doctrine of the Cognitive Illumination of the Holy Spirit as Developed in the Institutes of the Christian Religion." Unpublished dissertation, Western Conservative Baptist Seminary, 1977.

0102 Bartling, V. A. "Notes on Spirit-Baptism and Prophetic Utterance," *CTQ* 39 (November 1968): 708–14.

0103 Barton, John M. T. *The Holy Spirit.* Burns, Oates & Washbourne, 1930.

0104 Basham, Don. "Baptism in the Holy Spirit," in *The Holy Spirit in Today's Church,* Erling Jorstad, editor. Abingdon Press, 1973. Pp. 58–65.

0105 ______. *A Handbook on Holy Spirit Baptism.* Whitaker Books, 1969.

0106 Batdorf, Irvin W. "The Spirit of God in the Synoptic Gospels." Unpublished dissertation, Princeton Seminary, 1950.

0107 Bauckham, Richard J. "The Role of the Spirit in the Apocalypse," *EQ* 52 (April-June 1980): 66–83.

0108 Bavel, Tarcisius Jan van "Pinksteren en de overgang van de aardse Jezus naar de Christus van de verkondiging," in *Leven uit de geest.* Hilversum, 1974. Pp. 32–45.

0109 Bavinck, Johan H. *De Heilige Geest.* J. H. Kok, 1949.

0110 Beacham, Paul F. *Scriptural Sanctification.* Advocate Publishing House, n.d.

0111 Beasley-Murray, G. R. "The Holy Spirit, Baptism, and the Body of Christ," *RE* 63:2 (Spring 1966): 177–85.

0112 Becken, Hans-Jürgen. *Theologie der Heilung: Das Heilung in den Afrikanischen Unabhängigen Kirchen in Südafrika.* Verlag der Missionshandlung, 1972.

0113 Beckmann, Joachim. "Der Heilige Geist und die Heiligung," in *Im Kampf für die Kirche des Evangeliums,* Joachim Beckmann, editor. Gütersloher Verlagshaus Gerd Mohn, 1961. Pp. 64–74.

0114 ______. "Die Heilsnotwendigkeit der Taufe," in *Im Kampf für die Kirche des Evangeliums,* Joachim Beckmann, editor. Gütersloher Verlagshaus Gerd Mohn, 1961. Pp. 75–98.

0115 ______. "Recht und Grenze der Konfessionen," in *Im Kampf für die Kirche des Evangeliums,* Joachim Beckmann, editor. Gütersloher Verlagshaus Gerd Mohn, 1961. Pp. 60–63.

0116 Beeg, John F. "Belief and Values of Charismatics: A Survey." Unpublished dissertation, Colgate Rochester Divinity School, 1978.

0117 Behr-Sigel, Elisabeth. "La Place de la Femme dans l'Eglise" (2 parts), *Iren* 56:1 (1983): 46–53.

0118 Beker, Johan Christian. "Prophecy and the Spirit in the Apostolic Fathers." Unpublished dissertation, University of Chicago, 1955.

0119 Bellingham, John Alexander. "The Existential Relevance of the Holy Spirit of the Koinonia." Unpublished dissertation, Temple University, 1958.

0120 Benjamin, Harry S. "Pneuma in John and Paul: A Comparative Study of the Term with Particular Reference to the Holy Spirit," *BTB* 6 (Fall 1976): 27–48.

0121 Bender, Wolfgang. *Die Lehre über den Heiligen Geist bei Tertullian.* M. Hueber, 1961.

0122 Benner, Forest T. "The Immediate Antecedents of the Wesleyan Doctrine of the Witness of the Spirit." Unpublished dissertation, Temple University, 1966.

0123 Bennett, Dennis. "The Gifts of the Holy Spirit," in *The Charismatic Movement,* Michael Hamilton, editor. Eerdmans Publishing Co., 1975. Pp. 15–32.

0124 Bennett, Dennis and Rita Bennett. *The Holy Spirit and You.* Logos International, 1971.

0125 Bennett, E. Fay. "The Call of God in the Ministry of John Wesley: A Study in Methodist History." Unpublished dissertation, Southwestern Baptist Seminary, 1963.

0126 Benoit, A. "Le Saint-Esprit et l'église, dans la théologie patristique greque des quatre premiers siècles," in *L'Esprit Saint et L'Eglise.* Fayard, 1969. Pp. 125–41.

0127 Bense, Walter F. "Eastern Christianity in the Thought of Karl Holl," *UUC* 31:3–4 (Fall-Winter 1976): 3–4; 5–27.

0128 Benson, Alphonsus. *The Spirit of God in the Didactic Books of the Old Testament.* Catholic University of America Press, 1949.

0129 ______. "Spiritual and Moral Conditions of the Covenant People in the Time of Hosea." Unpublished dissertation, Grace Seminary, 1968.

0130 Benz, Ernst. *Der Heilige Geist in Amerika.* Diederichs, 1970.

0131 Berger, Alan L. "Hasidism and Moonism: Charisma in the Counterculture," *SA* 41 (Winter 1980): 375–90.

0132 Bergsma, Paul J. "The Homogeneous Unit Principle Debate: The Proposal, the Debate, and a Suggested Way Forward." Unpublished dissertation, Southwestern Baptist Seminary, 1982.

0133 Berkhof, Hendrikus. *The Doctrine of the Holy Spirit.* John Knox Press, 1964.

0134 ______. "De Geest als voorschot," in *Leven uit de geest.* Hilversum, 1974. Pp. 162–79.

0135 ______. "The Holy Spirit and the World: Some Reflections on Paul's Letter to the Colossians," *JTSA* (December 1979): 56–61.

0136 Berry, Donald Leroy. "The Holy Spirit and the Ministry of the Church." Unpublished dissertation, Yale University, 1959.

0137 Bertetto, Domenico. *Lo Spirito Santo e Santificatore.* Pro Sanctitate, 1977.

0138 Bertrams, Hermann. *Das Wesen des Geistes nach der Anschauung des Apostels Paulus.* Aschendorff, 1913.

0139 Besson, Henro. *Le mouvement de sanctification et le réveil d'Oxford.* Neuchâtel, 1914.

0140 Bethune, George W. *The Fruit of the Spirit.* J. Whetham, 1839.

0141 Betz, Otto. *Der Paraklet. Fürsprecher im häretischen Spätjudentum, im Johannes-Evangelium und in neu gefundenden gnostischen Schriften.* E. J. Brill, 1963.

0142 ______. "Die Proselytentaufe der Qumransekte und die Taufe im Neuen Testament," *RQu* 1 (October 1958): 213–34.

0143 Bezuidenhout, Marthinus Eduard Johannes. "Pauline Criteria Concerning the Practice of the Charismata: An Exegetical Study of 1 Cor 12–14." Unpublished dissertation, University of Pretoria, 1981.

0144 Bible, Ken. "The Wesleys' Hymns on Full Redemption and Pentecost: A Brief Comparison," *WTJ* 17 (Fall 1982): 79–87.

0145 Bickersteth, Edward Henry. *The Holy Spirit: His Person and Work.* Kregel, 1959.

0146 Biddulph, Thomas T. *Divine Influence: The Operation of the Holy Spirit Traced from the Creation of Man to the Consummation of All Things.* A. Brown, 1824.

0147 Biederwolf, William E. *A Help to the Study of the Holy Spirit.* J. H. Earle & Co., 1902.

0148 Bieritz, Karl H. "Abendmahlsverständnis und Abendmahlspraxis in der Gegenwart," *KD* 27 (October-December 1981): 242–68.

0149 Bilaniuk, Petro B. T. "The Holy Spirit in Eastern Christian Iconography," *PRZ* 1:2 (1982): 101–16.

0150 ______. "The Monk as Pneumatophor in the Writings of St. Basil the Great," *Diak* 15:1 (1980): 49–63.

0151 ______. "Some Remarks Concerning a Theological Description of Prayer," *GOTR* 21 (Fall 1976): 203–14.

0152 ______. *Theology and Economy of the Holy Spirit: An Eastern Approach.* Dharmaran Publications, 1980.

0153 ______. "The Theotokos as Pneumatophora," *JD* 5 (April-June 1980): 141–59.

0154 ______. "The Ultimate Reality and Meaning Expressed in Eastern Christian Icons," *UT* 5:4 (1982): 299–313.

0155 Bilolo, Mubabinge. "Die Begriffe 'Heiliger Geist' und 'Driefaltigkeit Gottes' angesichts der Afrikanischen Religiösen Überlieferung," *ZMR* 68 (January 1984): 1–23.

0156 Birch, Kenneth B. "Spiritual Gifts in Worship." Unpublished dissertation, Fuller Seminary, 1971.

0157 Bird, Thomas. "Experience Over Scripture in Charismatic Exegesis," *CTQ* 45 (January-April 1981): 5–11.

0158 Bishop, James R. *The Spirit of Christ in Human Relationships.* Zondervan, 1968.

0159 Bishop, William Samuel. *Christ and the Spirit: An Essay in New Testament Christology.* Longmans, Green & Co., 1941.

0160 Biskupek, Aloysius. *Come, Creator Spirit.* Mission Press, 1949.

0161 Bittlinger, Arnold. "Baptized in Water and in Spirit," in *The Gifts of the Spirit and the Body of Christ,* Elmo J. Agrimson, editor. Augsburg Publishing Co., 1974. Pp. 81–98.

0162 ______. "Charismatic Renewal: An Opportunity for the Church?" *EcR* 31:3 (July 1979): 247–51.

0163 ______. "A Charismatic Worship Service in the New Testament Today," *SL* 9:4 (1973): 215–29.

0164 Bittlinger, Arnold and Kilian McDonnell. *Baptism in the Holy Spirit as an Ecumenical Problem.* Charismatic Renewal Services, 1972.

0165 Blakemore, William Barnett. "Holy Spirit as Public and as Charismatic Institutions," *Enc* 36 (Summer 1975): 161–80.

0166 ______. "The Potentiality of Conciliarity: Communion, Conscience, Council," in *No Man is Alien,* J. Robert Nelson, editor. E. J. Brill, 1971. Pp. 225–44.

0167 Blaser, Klauspeter. "Segni della Speranza," *Prot* 35:3 (1980): 129–37.

0168 ______. *Vorstoß zur Pneumatologie.* Theologischer Verlag, 1977.

0169 Blauw, Johannes. *The Missionary Nature of the Church.* McGraw-Hill Book Co., 1962.

0170 Bloch-Hoell, Nils. "Den Heilige and I Pinsebevegelesen, den Charismatiske Beveglse og I Jesus-Vekkelsen," *NTT* 77:2 (1976): 75–86.

0171 ______. "Der Heilige Geist in der Pfingstbewegung und der charismatischen Bewegung," in *Taufe und Heiliger Geist,* Pertti Mäki, editor. Helsinki Press, 1979. Pp. 89–105.

0172 Blomfield, Charles James. *The Manifestation of the Spirit.* B. Fellowes, 1842.

0173 Blossom, Willis W. *The Gift of the Holy Spirit.* Privately published, 1925.

0174 Bloy, Myron B., Jr. *Search for the Sacred: The New Spiritual Quest.* Seabury Press, 1972.

0175 Bobrinskoy, Boris. "The Indwelling of the Spirit in Christ: 'Pneumatic Christology' in the Cappadocian Fathers," *SVTQ* 28:1 (1984): 49–65.

0176 ______. "Quelques réflexions sur la pneumatologie du culte," in *Le Saint-Esprit dans la Liturgie,* A. Pistoia and A. Triacca, editors. Bibliotheca Ephemerides Liturgicae, 1977. Pp. 29–38.

0177 Boehme, Armand J. "Sing a New Song: The Doctrine of Justification and the Lutheran Book of Worship Sacramental Liturgies," *CTQ* 43 (April 1979): 96–119.

0178 Boer, Harry R. *Pentecost and Missions.* Eerdmans Publishing Co., 1961.

0179 Bohen, Marian. "Confirmation: 'Mysterion' of the Holy Spirit. A Catechetical Study of the Second Sacrament of Christian Initiation." Unpublished dissertation, Catholic University of America, 1962.

0180 Bohne, Gerhard. " 'Nicht aus eigener Vernunft noch Kraft': Pädagogische Randbemerkungen zu Luthers Erklärung des III

Artikels," in *Ich Glaube Eine Heilige Kirche: H. Asmussen,* Walter Bauer, et al., editors. Evangelisches Verlag, 1963. Pp. 123–32.

0181 Boice, James M. *Awakening to God.* InterVarsity Press, 1979.

0182 Bomar, Joseph Washington. "The Relationship of the Holy Spirit to the Nature and Function of the Church in Contemporary Thought." Unpublished dissertation, Southwestern Seminary, 1960.

0183 Bona, Giovanni. *De Discretione spirituum liber unus.* L. Billaine, 1673.

0184 Bonnefoy, Jean François. *Le Saint-Esprit et ses dous selon saint Bonaventure.* Vrin, 1929.

0185 Bonner, Gerald. " 'The Holy Spirit Within': St. Cuthbert as a Western Orthodox Saint," *Sob* 1:1 (1979): 7–22.

0186 Boring, M. Eugene. "Influence of Christian Prophecy on the Johannine Portrayal of the Paraclete and Jesus," *NTS* 25 (October 1978): 113–23.

0187 Bornkamm, Günther. "Der Paraklet im Johannesevangelium," in *Festschrift Rudolf Bultmann zum 65. Geburtstag überreicht.* Kohlhammer, 1949. Pp. 12–35.

0188 Boros, Ladislaus. "Discernment of the Spirit," in *Charisms in the Church,* Christian Duquoc and Casiano Floristan, editors. Seabury Press, 1978. Pp. 78–86.

0189 Bosch, F. W. A. "The Holy Spirit." Unpublished dissertation, Temple University, 1940.

0190 Bouchet, Jean-René. "The Discernment of Spirits," in *Conflicts about the Holy Spirit,* Hans Küng and Jürgen Moltmann, editors. Seabury Press, 1979. Pp. 103–10.

0191 Bourassa, François. " 'Dans la Communion de L'Esprit Saint': Etude Théologique" (part 1), *SEs* 34 (January-April 1982): 31–56.

0192 ______. " 'Dans la Communion de L'Esprit Saint': Etude Théologique" (part 2), *SEs* 34 (May-September 1982): 135–49.

0193 ______. "Esprit Saint, 'Communion' du Père et du Fils," *SEs* 30 (January-April 1978): 5–37.

0194 ______. "Sur la Propriété de L'Esprit Saint, Questions Disputees" (part 1), *SEs* 28 (October-December 1976): 243–64.

0195 ______. "Sur la Propriété de L'Esprit Saint, Questions Disputees" (part 2), *SEs* 29 (January-April 1977): 23–43.

0196 Bouyer, Louis. *Le Consolateur: Esprit-Saint et vie de Grace.* Les Editions du Cerf, 1980.

0197 ______. "Eucharistic Celebration and Prayer in the Spirit," *DR* 95: (July 1977): 214–25.

0198 Bowen, T. M. *Why We Baptize in Jesus' Name.* Pentecostal Publishing House, n.d.

0199 Bower, Robert K. *Biblical and Psychological Perspectives for Christian Counselors.* William Carey Library, 1974.

0200 Boyack, Alice S. "Evelyn Underhill's Interpretation of the Spiritual Life." Unpublished dissertation, University of Chicago, 1964.

0201 Boyd, Frank M. *The Holy Spirit: Teacher's Manual.* Gospel Publishing House, n.d.

0202 Boyer, Harold W. "The Holy Spirit in the Believer and the Church," in *Dynamics of the Faith,* Gene Miller, Max Gaulke, Donald Smith, editors. Gulf-Coast Bible College, 1972. Pp. 181–96.

0203 Braaten, Carl E. "Spirituality of Hope," in *Christ and Counter-Christ: Apocalyptic Themes in Theology and Culture.* Fortress Press, 1972. Pp. 82–100.

0204 Bracança, Joaquim O. "L'Esprit Saint dans l'euchologie médiévale," in *Le Saint-Esprit dans la Liturgie,* A. Pistoia and A. Triacca, editors. Bibliotheca Ephemerides Liturgicae, 1977. Pp. 39–53.

0205 Bradford, Amory H. *Spirit and Life.* Pilgrim Press, 1888.

0206 Bradford, Rick. *Releasing the Power of the Holy Spirit.* Charismatic Communion, 1983.

0207 Brand, Paul, et al., eds. *Experience de L'Esprit: Mélanges E. Schillebeeckx.* Beauchesne, 1976.

0208 Brandt, Wilfried. *Der Heilige Geist und die Kirche bei Schleiermacher.* Zwingli Verlag, 1968.

0209 Branick, Vincent P. *Mary, the Spirit and the Church.* Paulist Press, 1980.

0210 Branner, John E. "Roland Allen: Pioneer in a Spirit-Centered Theology of Mission," *M* 5 (April 1977): 175–84.

0211 Branson, William Henry. *The Holy Spirit: His Office and Work in the World.* N.p., n.d.

0212 Bray, Gerald. "The Filioque Clause in History and Theology," *TB* 34 (1983): 91–144.

0213 Bray, John L. *The Holy Spirit in the Life of the Christian.* Privately published, 1971.

0214 Brazer, John. *Essay on the Doctrine of Divine Influence upon the Human Soul.* Munroe, 1835.

0215 Breck, John. "Exegesis and Interpretation: Orthodox Reflections on the 'Hermeneutic Problem,' " *SVTQ* 27:2 (1983): 75–92.

0216 Bredow, Gerda von. "Der Geist als lebendiges Bild Gottes," in *Das Menschenbild des Nikolaus von Kues,* Martin Bodweig, et al., editors. Matthias-Grünewald-Verlag, 1978. Pp. 58–67.

0217 Brengle, Samuel L. *When the Holy Ghost Is Come.* Salvationist Publishing & Supplies, 1954.

0218 Bresson, Bernard L. *Studies in Ecstasy.* Vantage Press, 1966.

0219 Breton, Valentin. *The Blessed Trinity: History, Theology, Spirituality.* Sands & Company, 1934.

0220 Bridge, Donald and David Phypers. *Spiritual Gifts and the Church.* InterVarsity Press, 1973.

0221 Briggs, C. A. "The Use of *Ruah* in the Old Testament," *JBL* 19 (1900): 132–45.

0222 Bright, Bill. *The Holy Spirit: The Key to Supernatural Living.* Here's Life Publishers, 1980.

0223 Brightman, Edgar Sheffield. *The Spiritual Life.* Abingdon-Cokesbury, 1942.

0224 Bristol, Sherlock. *Paracletos: The Baptism of the Holy Ghost.* Revell Co., 1892.

0225 Brock, Sebastian P. *The Holy Spirit in the Syrian Baptismal Tradition.* Deepika Book Stall, 1979.

0226 ______. "Passover, Annunciation and Epiclesis: Some Remarks on the Term Aggen in the Syriac Versions of Lk 1:35," *NT* 24 (July 1982): 222–23.

0227 Broer, I. "Der Geist und die Gemeinde," *BL* 13 (1972): 261–83.

0228 Brookes, James H. *The Holy Spirit.* Gospel Book and Tract Depository, n.d.

0229 Broomall, Wick. *The Holy Spirit: A Scriptural Study of His Person and Work.* Baker Book House, 1963.

0230 Brown, Charles C. *The Meaning of Sanctification.* Warner Press, 1945.

0231 Brown, Dale W. "Biblical Distinctiveness, the Brethren, and Union," *BLT* 11:1 (Winter 1966): 45–51.

0232 ______. *Flamed by the Spirit: Biblical Definition of the Holy Spirit.* New Zealand Press, 1980.

0233 Brown, George Thompson. "The Relation Between Christ and the Holy Spirit in the Pauline Epistles." Unpublished thesis, Princeton Seminary, 1950.

0234 Brown, John E. *The Work of the Spirit.* International Federation Publishing Co., n.d.

0235 Brown, Raymond E. "Diverse Views of the Spirit in the New Testament," *Wor* 57 (May 1983): 225–36.

0236 ______. "The Paraclete in the Fourth Gospel," *NTS* 13 (1966–67): 113–32.

0237 Brown, Ronald P. "Gifts of the Holy Spirit," *RefR* 28 (Spring 1975): 171–82.

0238 Brown, Schuyler. "Water-Baptism and Spirit-Baptism in Luke–Acts," *ATR* 59 (April 1977): 135–51.

0239 Brownville, C. C. *Symbols of the Holy Spirit.* Revell Co., 1940.

0240 Bruce, F. F. "The Spirit in the Letter to the Galatians," in *Essays on Apostolic Themes: Studies in Honor of Howard M. Ervin.* Paul Elbert, editor. Hendrickson Publishers, 1985. Pp. 36–48.

0241 Bruner, Frederick Dale. "The Doctrine and Experience of the Holy Spirit in the Pentecostal Movement and Correspondingly in the New Testament." Unpublished dissertation, University of Hamburg, 1963.

0242 ______. "The Holy Spirit: Conceiver of Jesus," in *Ecumenism and Vatican II,* Pedro S. de Achutegui, editor. Ateneo de Manila University, 1972. Pp. 64–74.

0243 ______. *A Theology of the Holy Spirit: The Pentecostal Experience and the New Testament.* Eerdmans Publishing Co., 1970.

0244 Bruner, Frederick Dale and William Hordern. *The Holy Spirit: Shy Member of the Trinity.* Augsburg Publishing Co., 1984.

0245 Brunk, George R. *Encounter with the Holy Spirit (Consultation on the Person and Work of the Holy Spirit, Eastern Mennonite College, January 1972).* Herald Press, 1972.

0246 ______. "The Holy Spirit in Exaltation of Christ," in *Encounter with the Holy Spirit,* George R. Brunk, II, editor. Herald Press, 1972. Pp. 7–15.

0247 Brunner, Heinrich Emil. *Die Lehre vom Heiligen Geiste.* Zwingli Verlag, 1945.

0248 ______. *Vom Werk des Heiligen Geistes.* Mohr, 1935.

0249 Bruton, James Redd. "The Concept of the Holy Spirit as a Theological Motif in Luke–Acts." Unpublished dissertation, Southern Baptist Seminary, 1967.

0250 Brylinski, Jean D. "Bible A.T. Elle Remplace le Ressuscité," *ETR* 53:3 (1978): 416–19.

0251 Buchanan, Colin. "Baptism in the Holy Spirit," *Chm* 86 (1972): 39–46.

0252 Buchanan, James. *The Office and Work of the Holy Spirit.* Hamilton, Adams and Co., 1857.

0253 Bugbee, Lucius Hatfield. *The Divine Presence: A Study of the Holy Spirit.* The Methodist Book Concern, 1930.

0254 Bulgakov, Serger Nikolaevich. *Le Paraclet.* Aubier, 1946.

0255 Bull, Paul Bertie. *The Spirit of Wisdom, Love, and Power.* N.p., 1928.

0256 Bullinger, Ethelbert W. *The Giver and His Gifts.* Lamp Press, 1953.

0257 ______. *The Holy Spirit and His Work.* Kregel, 1979.

0258 Bullock, Charles. *The Forgotten Truth: The Gospel of the Holy Spirit.* N.p., n.d.

0259 Bunn, John T. "Glossolalia in Historical Perspective," in *Speaking in Tongues: Let's Talk About It,* Watson E. Mills, editor. Word Books, 1973. Pp. 36–47.

0260 Burgess, Stanley M. *The Spirit and the Church: Antiquity.* Hendrickson, 1984.

0261 Buri, Fritz. "Trinity and Personality," *IR* 40 (Winter 1983): 15–24.

0262 Burks, Robert E. "Jesus and the Spirit in the Synoptic Gospels." Unpublished dissertation, Southern Baptist Seminary, 1961.

0263 Burleigh, J. H. S. "The Doctrine of the Holy Spirit in the Latin Fathers," *SJT* 7 (1954): 113–32.

0264 Burnett, Bill. "The Spirit and Social Action," in *Bishop's Move,* Michael Harper, editor. Hodder & Stoughton, 1978. Pp. 27–59.

0265 Burns, James A. "The Phenomenology of the Holy Spirit." Unpublished dissertation, Marquette University, 1968.

0266 Burns, Lanier. "Reemphasis on the Purpose of the Sign Gifts," *BS* 132 (July-September 1975): 242–49.

0267 Burns, J. Patout and Gerald M. Fagin, *The Holy Spirit.* Michael Glazier, 1984.

0268 Burroughs, Prince Emanuel. *The Holy Spirit and the Believer.* Privately published, 1898.

0269 Burrow, Reuben. *A Discourse on Christian Baptism.* Banner of Peace, 1845.

0270 Burtner, Robert W. and Robert E. Chiles. *A Compendium of Wesley's Theology.* Abingdon Press, 1954.

0271 Burton, Edward. *Testimonies of the Ante-Nicene Fathers to the Doctrine of the Trinity and of the Divinity of the Holy Ghost.* Oxford University Press, 1831.

0272 Butler, Basil C. "God's Kingdom: Future or Present," *DR* 95 (July 1977): 164–75.

0273 Byrne, James. *Threshold of God's Promise: An Introduction to the Catholic Pentecostal Movement.* Ave Maria Press, 1970.

0274 Byrum, Russel R. *Holy Spirit Baptism and the Second Cleansing.* Gospel Trumpet Co., 1923.

C

0275 Caffarel, Henri. *Faut-il parler d'un pentecôtisme catholique?* Editions du Feu Nouveau, 1973.

0276 Cafone, James Michael. "The Role of the Holy Spirit in the Theology of Charles Grandison Finney." Unpublished dissertation, Catholic University of America, 1979.

0277 Caldwell, Georgine Granger. "Toward a Theology of the Laity in Christian Religious Education." Unpublished dissertation, Columbia University Teacher's College, 1980.

0278 Caldwell, William. *Pentecostal Baptism.* Miracle Moments Evangelistic Association, 1963.

0279 Calkins, Raymond. *The Holy Spirit.* Abingdon Press, 1930.

0280 Camelot, Pierre-Thomas. "God: A Spirit Who Makes One Live," in *Moral Formation and Christianity,* Franz Bockle and Jacques-Marie Pohier, editors. Seabury Press, 1978. Pp. 21–28.

0281 Camfield, F. W. *Revelation and the Holy Spirit.* Elliott Stock, 1933.

0282 Campbell, A. "The Influence of the Holy Spirit on Conversion and Sanctification," in *A Symposium on the Holy Spirit.* John Burns, 1879. Pp. 116–55.

0283 Campbell, James M. *After Pentecost, What? A Discussion of the Doctrine of the Holy Spirit in Its Relation to Modern Christological Thought.* Revell Co., 1897.

0284 Campbell, Joseph H. *Warning! Do Not Seek for Tongues: A Sound Scriptural Appraisal of a Present-Day Trend in the Church.* World Outlook Publications, 1970.

0285 Campbell, T. "The Doctrine of the Holy Spirit in the Theology of Athanasius," *SJT* 27 (1974): 408–40.

0286 Canart, P. "Nicephore Blemmyde et le Memoire Adresse Aux Envoyes de Gregoire IX," *OCP* 25 (1959): 310–25.

0287 Candal, Manuel. "La 'Apologia' del Plusiadeno a Favor del Concilio de Florencia," *OCP* 21 (1955): 36–57.

0288 Candlish, James S. *The Work of the Holy Spirit.* T. & T. Clark, 1886.

0289 Cannon, William R. "The Holy Spirit in the Godhead," *OC* 16:3 (1980): 169–84.

0290 ______. *The Theology of John Wesley.* Abingdon Press, 1946.

0291 Cantelon, Willard. *The Baptism of the Holy Spirit.* Gospel Publishing House, 1957.

0292 Cargas, Harry J. and Bernard Lee. *Religious Experience and Process Theology: The Pastoral Implications of a Major Modern Movement.* Paulist Press, 1976.

0293 Carlson, Arnold E. "The Relevance of Luther's Understanding of the Holy Spirit for Contemporary Theology." Unpublished dissertation, Union Seminary, New York, 1962.

0294 Carlson, Charles H. *Dry Bones Can Live: A Plan for Renewal and Growth.* First Presbyterian Church, Billingham, Washington, 1986.

0295 Carr, Wesley. "Towards a Contemporary Theology of the Holy Spirit," *SJT* 28:6 (1975): 501–16.

0296 Carrillo, Alday Salvador. "Baptism in the Holy Spirit: Theological and Pastoral Questions," in *Spirit and the Church,* Ralph Martin, compiler. Pentecostal Publishing House, 1977. Pp. 182–91.

0297 Carroll, B. H. *The Holy Spirit.* Zondervan, 1939.

0298 Carson, Donald A. "The Function of the Paraclete in John 16:7–11," *JBL* 98 (December 1979): 547–66.

0299 Carter, Charles W. *The Bible Gift of Tongues.* Wesleyan Methodist Publishing Company, 1954.

0300 ______. *The Person and Ministry of the Holy Spirit.* Baker Book House, 1974.

0301 ______. *Road to Revival.* Higley Press, 1959.

0302 ______. "A Wesleyan View of the Spirit's Gift of Tongues in the Book of Acts," *WTJ* (Spring 1969): 39–68.

0303 Carter, Howard. *The Gifts of the Spirit.* Northern Gospel Publishing House, 1946.

0304 Carter, James E. "The Tongues of Pentecost," *BI* 13:3 (1987): 29–31.

0305 Cartwright, Christine. "Charismatic Culture in St. John's, Newfoundland: A Cross-Denominational Study of Religious Folklife in Three Groups." Unpublished dissertation, Memorial University of Newfoundland, 1983.

0306 Cartwright, Colbert S. "The Spiritual Nature of the Church," *MSt* 19 (July 1980): 322–33.

0307 Cary, Clement C. *The Witness of the Spirit.* N.p., n.d.

0308 Cash, William Wilson. *In the Power of the Spirit.* Church Missionary Society, 1948.

0309 Cassese, Michele. "Die Ekklesiologie der 'Confessio Augustana,'" *Cat* 34:4 (1980): 296–333.

0310 Cassidy, Michael. "The Promise of the Father (in South Africa)," *JTSA* 29 (December 1979): 14–22.

0311 Casurella, Anthony. *The Johannine Paraclete in the Church Fathers.* Mohr, 1983.

0312 Cattell, Everett Lewis. *The Spirit of Holiness.* Eerdmans Publishing Co., 1963.

0313 Caudill, R. Paul. *Modern Acts of the Holy Spirit.* Broadman Press, 1982.

0314 Cavanaugh, Joseph H. "The Regulation of the Gifts of the Holy Spirit." Unpublished dissertation, University of Laval, 1947.

0315 Cayley, Murray A. *Are We Spiritually Dead?* The Stratford Company, 1932.

0316 Cazelles, Henri. *Le mystère de l'Esprit Saint.* Mame, 1968.

0317 Cell, G. C. *The Rediscovery of John Wesley.* Henry Holt & Company, 1935.

0318 Cennick, John. *The Gift and Office of the Holy Ghost.* Paternoster, 1771.

0319 Cerfaux, Lucien. "Simples Refléxions A Propos de L'Exégèse Apostolique," *ETL* 25 (1949): 565–76.

0320 Chadwick, Samuel. *The Way to Pentecost.* Light & Hope Publications, 1937.

0321 Chafer, Lewis Sperry. "The Baptism of the Holy Spirit," *BS* 109 (1952): 199–216.

0322 Chambers, D. "Doctrinal Attitudes in the Church of Scotland in the Pre-Disruption Era: The Age of John McLeod Campbell and Edward Irving," *JRH* 8 (December 1974): 159–82.

0323 Champion, L. G. "The Baptist Doctrine of the Church in Relation to Scripture, Tradition, and the Holy Spirit," *Found* 2 (1959): 27–39.

0324 Chang, Dong-Chan. "The Doctrine of the Holy Spirit in the Thought of the Cappadocian Fathers." Unpublished dissertation, Drew University, 1983.

0325 Chapman, J. B. *The Terminology of Holiness.* Beacon Hill Press, 1947.

0326 Chapman, J. Wilbur. *Receive Ye the Holy Spirit.* Revell Co., 1894.

0327 Cheney, John R. "Luke's Use of the Expression 'The Holy Spirit': Its Bearing upon the Problem of His Sources." Unpublished dissertation, Boston University, 1928.

0328 Chenu, Marie-Dominique. "Evangelisch reveil en aanwezigheid van de Geest in de 12e en 13e eeuw," in *Leven uit de geest.* Hilversum, 1974. Pp. 145–49.

0329 Cheshire, C. Linwood, Jr. "The Doctrine of the Holy Spirit in the Acts." Unpublished thesis, Union Seminary in Virgina, 1953.

0330 Chevallier, Max A. *L'Esprit et le Messie dans le bas-judaisme et le Nouveau Testament.* Presses Universitaires de France, 1958.

0331 ______. "L'Evangile de Jean et le 'Filique' (Jn 15:26)," *RSciRel* 57 (April 1983): 93–111.

0332 ______. "Luc et l'Esprit Saint: A la Memoire du P. Augustin George (1915–1977)," *RSciRel* 56 (January 1982): 1–16.

0333 ______. " 'Pentecôtes' Lucaniennes et 'Pentecôtes' Johanniques," *ReSR* 69 (April-June 1981): 301–13.

0334 Christenson, Larry. "Pentecostalism's Forgotten Forerunner," in *Aspects of Pentecostal-Charismatic Origins,* Vinson Synan, editor. Logos International, 1975. Pp. 15–37.

0335 ______. *Speaking in Tongues and Its Significance for the Church.* Bethany, 1968.

0336 "Christian Witness: A Theological Study" (trans. by the WCC Language Service), *IntRMiss* 69 (April 1980): 121–34.

0337 Chung, Hwan Kwak. *Outline of the Principle: Level 4.* Holy Spirit Association for the Unification of World Christianity, 1980.

0338 *Church Studies on the Holy Spirit,* (documents from the Presbyterian Church of the USA, Church of Scotland, and Presbyterian Church of Canada). Council on Theology and Culture, 1978.

0339 Clapsis, Emmanuel. "The Filioque Question," *PRZ* 2:1 (1982): 127–36.

0340 Clark, Adam. *Entire Sanctification: The Twelfth Chapter of Clarke's Christian Theology.* Pentecostal Publishing House, n.d.

0341 Clark, Charles Barton. "A Reinvestigation of Mark 13 as a Possible Key to the Structure of the Gospel." Unpublished dissertation, Southwestern Baptist Seminary, 1981.

0342 Clark, Dougan. *The Holy Ghost Dispensation.* Revell Co., 1891.

0343 ______. *The Offices of the Holy Spirit.* National Publishing House, 1879.

0344 Clark, Elijah C. *The Baptism of the Holy Ghost "And More."* Church of God Publishing House, 1931.

0345 Clark, Glenn. *The Holy Spirit.* Macalester Publishing Company, 1956.

0346 Clark, Ian D. L. "Ananda (Concepts of Joy, Bliss, and Spirit in Christianity and Hinduism)," *TH* 86 (January 1983): 15–19.

0347 Clark, J. P. H. "Walter Hilton and 'Liberty of Spirit,' " *DR* 96 (January 1978): 61–78.

0348 Clark, Stephen. *Confirmation and the "Baptism of the Holy Spirit."* Dove Publications, 1969.

0349 ______. *Spiritual Gifts.* Dove Publications, 1969.

0350 Clark, William R. *The Paraclete: A Series of Discourses on the Person and Work of the Holy Spirit.* T. & T. Clark, 1900.

0351 Claybrook, Donald A. "The Emerging Doctrine of the Holy Spirit in the Writings of Jürgen Moltmann." Unpublished dissertation, Southern Baptist Seminary, 1983.

0352 Clemance, Clement. *The Scripture Doctrine of the Holy Spirit.* John Snow and Company, 1887.

0353 Clément, O. "A propos de l'Esprit-Saint," *Con* 26 (1974): 85–91.

0354 Clements, Keith W. "Atonement and the Holy Spirit," *ExT* 95 (March 1984): 168–71.

0355 Clymer, Wayne Kenton. *Membership Means Discipleship.* Discipleship Resources, 1976.

0356 Cockin, Frederick Arthur. *God in Action: A Study in the Holy Spirit.* Penguin Books, 1961.

0357 ______. *The Holy Spirit and the Church.* SCM Press, 1939.

0358 Cocks, H. F. Lovell. "The Communion of the Holy Spirit (Sermon, Whitsunday; 2 Cor 13:14)," *ExT* 68 (May 1957): 249–51.

0359 Cocoris, Michael. "Speaking in Tongues: Then and Now," *BRQ* 46:6 (September 1981): 14–16.

0360 Coetzee, J. C. "The Holy Spirit in 1 John," in *Studies in the Johannine Letters,* J. Rand, et al., editors. Tidings Publishing Co., 1981. Pp. 30–41.

0361 Cohn Werner. "Personality and Pentecostal Groups: A Research Note." Unpublished paper, University of British Columbia, 1967.

0362 Coke, Thomas and Henry Moore. *Life of the Rev. John Wesley, Including an Account of the Great Revival of Religion in Europe and America of Which He was the First and Chief Instrument.* G. Paramore, 1972.

0363 Coleman, Lyman. *Holy Spirit: Come, Holy Spirit.* Abingdon Press, 1981.

0364 Coleman, Robert. *The Spirit and the Word.* Asbury Theological Seminary 1965.

0365 Colilli, Paul Anthony. "Petrarch's Theology of the Veil." Unpublished dissertation, University of Toronto, 1983.

0366 Collier, F. W. *John Wesley Among the Scientists.* Abingdon Press, 1928.

0367 Collins, Adela Yarbro. "The Function of Excommunication in Paul," *HTR* 73 (January-April 1980): 251–63.

0368 Colpe, Carsten. "Der Spruch von der Lästerung des Geistes," in *Der Ruf Jesu und die Antwort der Gemeinde,* Eduard Lohse, editor. Vandenhoeck & Ruprecht, 1970. Pp. 63–79.

0369 Colwell, E. C. and Eric L. Titus. *The Gospel of the Spirit.* Harper & Brothers, 1953.

0370 Combet, Georges and Laureat Fabre. "The Pentecostal Movement and the Gift of Healing," in *Healing and the Spirit,* Georges Combet and Laureat Fabre, editors. Seabury Press, 1974. Pp. 106–10.

0371 Comblin, Joseph. *O Espirito no mundo.* Editora Vozes, 1978.

0372 Come, Arnold B. *Human Spirit and Holy Spirit.* Westminster Press, 1959.

0373 "The Communion of the Holy Spirit Today: Trinity, Church, Creation (report of Conference of European Churches, Cardiff, 1981; occasional paper 13)," *OC* 18:2 (1982): 177–80.

0374 Conde, Emilio. "La pneumatologie dans la théologie catholique," *RSPT* 51 (1972): 250–58.

0375 Congar, Yves M. "Blasphemy Against the Holy Spirit," in *Experience of the Spirit,* Peter Huizing and William Bassett. Seabury Press, 1974. Pp. 47–57.

0376 ______. "Chronique de Pneumatologie," *RSPT* 64 (July 1980): 445–51.

0377 ______. "Diversité de Dogmatique dans l'Unité de Foi entre Orient et Occident: Pour le Centenaire du Concile de 381," *Iren* 54:1 (1981): 25–35.

0378 ______. *Esquisses du mystère de l'église.* Les Editions du Cerf, 1953.

0379 ______. "De lastering tegen de Heilge Geest," in *Leven uit de geest.* Hilversum, 1974. Pp. 17–31.

0380 ______. "Pour une Christologie Pneumatologique: Note Bibliographique," *RSPT* 63 (July 1979): 435–42.

0381 ______. "Renouveau dans l'Esprit et Institution Ecclésiale: Mutuelle Interrogation," *RHPR* 55:1 (1975): 143–56.

0382 Congar, Yves M., with David Smith (trans.). *I Believe in the Holy Spirit.* 3 vols. Seabury Press, 1983.

0383 Conklin, James Ernest. "Worldview Evangelism: A Case Study of the Karen Baptist Church in Thailand." Unpublished dissertation, Fuller Seminary, 1984.

0384 Conn, Charles W. *Like a Mighty Army, Moves the Church of God.* Church of God Publishing House, 1955.

0385 ______. *A Balanced Church.* Pathway Press, 1975.

0386 Connelly, James T. "Not in Reputable Churches? The Reception of the Charismatic Movement in the Mainline Churches of America," in *Essays on Apostolic Themes: Studies in Honor of Howard M. Ervin.* Paul Elbert, editor. Hendrickson Publishers, 1985. Pp. 184–92.

0387 Conner, Walter Thomas. *The Work of the Holy Spirit.* Broadman Press, 1949.

0388 Constantelos, Demetrios J. "Toward the Convocation of the Second Ecumenical Synod," *GOTR* 27 (Winter 1982): 395–405.

0389 Cook, Clyde. "Cross-Cultural Persuasive Evangelism: A Study of Selected Early and Contemporary Christian Models." Unpublished dissertation, Fuller Seminary, 1974.

0390 Cook, Thomas. *New Testament Holiness.* Epworth, n.d.

0391 Cooper, John Charles. "The Significance of the Pauline Spirit: Christology for the Doctrine of the Spiritual Presence in the Theology of Paul Tillich." Unpublished dissertation, University of Chicago, 1967.

0392 Cope, Frederick J. *Tarry.* Pentecostal Publishing House, 1909.

0393 Copley, A. S. *The Holy Spirit: The One Baptism, the Anointing, Personal and Practical.* Grace and Glory, n.d.

0394 Coppedge, Allan. "Holiness and Discipleship," *WTJ* 15 (Fall 1980): 80–97.

0395 Coppens, Joseph C., et al., eds. *Ecclesia A Spiritu Santo Edocta: Mélanges théologiques Hommage A. Mgr Gerard Philips.* J. Duculot, 1970.

0396 Corbin, Michel. "De l'Impossible en Dieu: Lecture du 8E Chapitre du Dialogue de Saint Anselme sur la Liberté (on Free Choice; Proslogion, ch 7)," *RSPT* 66 (October 1982): 523–50.

0397 Corcoran, Patrick. "The Holy Spirit and the Life of the Spirit Today," in *Witness to the Spirit: Essays on Revelation, Spirit, Redemption,* Wilfrid Harrington, editor. Koinonia Press, 1979. Pp. 97–111.

0398 Corlett, S. Shelby. *The Baptism with the Holy Spirit.* Nazarene Publishing House, n.d.

0399 Cotty, Marion. "Paul and the Spirit." Unpublished thesis, Emory University, 1978.

0400 Courtney, Charles, Olin M. Ivey, and Gordon E. Michalson. *Hermeneutics and the Worldliness of Faith: A Festschrift in Memory of Carl Michaelson.* Drew University, 1974.

0401 Cowan, Arthur A. "How Dead Certainties Come Alive (Sermon, Whitsunday; Ezek 37:3, 2 Cor 13:14)," *ExT* 60 (May 1949): 221–23.

0402 ______. "Is It Illusion or Inspiration (Sermon, 1st Sunday After Trinity: 1 Cor 12:3)?" *ExT* 68 (May 1957): 252–53.

0403 Cox, Leo G. *John Wesley's Concept of Perfection.* Beacon Hill Press, 1964.

0404 Coyle, J. P. *The Spirit in Literature and Life.* Houghton, Mifflin & Company, 1896.

0405 Crain, Charles E. "The Significance of Paul's Teaching on the Holy Spirit for a Christian View of Man." Unpublished dissertation, Drew University, 1951.

0406 Craker, Wendel D. "Holy Spirit and Human Personality," *JPTh* 4 (Fall 1976): 269–79.

0407 Cramer, Winfrid. *Der Geist Gottes und des Menschen in frühsyrischer Theologie.* Aschendorff, 1979.

0408 Cramer, Wolfgang. *Grundlegung einer Theorie des Geistes.* Vittorio Kostermann, 1957.

0409 Crane, Louis Burton. *The Teachings of Jesus Concerning the Holy Spirit.* American Tract Society, 1905.

0410 Crehan, Joseph H. "Eucharistic Epiklesis: New Evidence and a New Theory," *ThSt* 41 (December 1980): 698–712.

0411 Cremer, A. H. "Charismata," in *The New Schaff-Herzog Encyclopedia of Religious Knowledge,* S. M. Jackson, editor. 13 vols. Baker Book House, 1950. 3:11.

0412 Crichton, J. D. "The Holy Spirit in Eucharistic Celebration," in *Pastoral Liturgy,* Harold Winstone, editor. Collins, 1975. Pp. 15–29.

0413 Criswell, W. A. *The Baptism, Filling and Gifts of the Holy Spirit.* Zondervan, 1973.

0414 ______. *The Holy Spirit in Today's World.* Zondervan, 1966.

0415 Cron, George. *The Holy Spirit's Work: Its Nature and Extent.* Hamilton, Adams & Company, 1880.

0416 Crow, Paul A. "Holy Spirit and the Unity of Christ's Church (Acts 2:11)," *PSB* 68 (Autumn 1975): 60–63.

0417 Crowe, Frederick E. "Son and Spirit: Tension in the Divine Missions (French Summary)," *SEs* 35 (May-October 1983): 153–69.

0418 Crump, Francis Joseph. *Pneuma in the Gospels.* Catholic University of America Press, 1954.

0419 Cubie, David L. "Perfection in Wesley and Fletcher: Inaugural or Teleological," *WTJ* 11 (Spring 1976): 22–37.

0420 Cubine, Margaret Virginia. "John Calvin's Doctrine of the Work of the Holy Spirit Examined in the Light of Some Contemporary Theories of Interpersonal Psychotherapy." Unpublished dissertation, Northwestern University, 1955.

0421 Cullmann, Oscar. "Holy Spirit and Critique," *IR* 36 (Winter 1979): 5–9.

0422 ______. "La Prière selon les Epîtres Pauliniennes: Conference Donnee à l'Universite d'Athenes le 11 Mai 1978," *ThZ* 35 (March-April 1979): 90–101.

0423 Cully, Iris V. "Continuity and Process in Religious Education," *LTQ* 12 (January 1977): 15–22.

0424 Cuming, Geoffrey J. "New Testament Foundation for Common Prayer," *SL* 10:3–4 (1974): 88–105.

0425 Cumming, James E. *Through the Eternal Spirit: A Biblical Study on the Holy Ghost.* Revell Co., 1896.

0426 Cumming, John. *The Comforter: Thoughts on the Influence of the Holy Spirit.* Hall & Virtue, 1854.

0427 Cummings, Crest Raymond. "Water Baptism and the Reception of the Holy Spirit: A Study in the Acts of the Apostles and the Early Church Fathers." Unpublished thesis, Oral Roberts University, 1978.

0428 Cunliffe-Jones, Hubert. *The Holy Spirit.* Independent Press, 1943.

0429 Cunningham, Richard B. *The Witness Within.* Sunday School Board, 1971.

0430 Custeau, J. and R. Michael. *Reconnaître l'Esprit.* Privately published, 1974.

0431 Cutler, S. *The Work of the Spirit.* American Tract Society, 1873.

D

0432 Daecke, Sigurd M. "Gott—Opfer oder Schöpfer der Evolution: Christlicher Glaube und Entwicklungslehre," *KD* 28 (October-December 1982): 230–47.

0433 Dagens, Claude. *Le maître de l'impossible: l'Esprit Saint, l'homme et l'Eglise.* Fayard, 1982.

0434 Dail, Francis Roderick. "The Holy Spirit and Christian Education." Unpublished dissertation, Columbia University, 1958.

0435 Dalmais, Irenee H. "L'Esprit Saint et le mystère du salut dans les épiclèses eucharistiques syriennes," in *Le Saint-Esprit dans la Liturgie,* A. Pistoia and A. Triacca, editors. Bibliotheca Ephemerides Liturgicae, 1977. Pp. 39–53.

0436 Dana, H. E. *The Holy Spirit in Acts.* Central Seminary Press, 1943.

0437 Daneel, Marthinus L. "Charismatic Healing in African Independent Churches," *ThEv* 16:3 (1983): 27–44.

0438 Daniélou, Jean. "Onction et Baptême chez Grégorie de Nysse," in *Le Saint-Esprit dans la Liturgie,* A. Pistoia and A. Triacca, editors. Bibliotheca Ephemerides Liturgicae, 1977. Pp. 65–70.

0439 Danker, Frederick W. "Shape of Luke's Gospel in Lectionaries," *Int* 30 (October 1976): 339–52.

0440 Dart, John. "Balancing Out the Trinity: The Genders of the Godhead," *ChrCent* 100 (February 1983): 147–50.

0441 Daunt, Achilles. *The Person and Offices of the Holy Spirit.* Hodder & Stoughton, 1879.

0442 Davies, G. Henton. "The Holy Spirit in the Old Testament," *RE* 63:2 (Spring 1966): 129–34.

0443 Davies, J. G. "The Primary Meaning of PARAKLETOS," *JTS* 4 (1953): 35–38.

0444 ______. *The Spirit, the Church, and the Sacraments.* Faith Press, 1954.

0445 Davies, J. Hywell. *The Renewal of the Church from a Pentecostal Viewpoint.* World Council of Churches, 1966.

0446 Davis, Edward. *The Gift of the Holy Ghost: The Believer's Privilege.* Privately published, 1874.

0447 Davison, John A. "Freedom of Thought and the Spirit of Hierarchy." Unpublished dissertation, Southern Baptist Seminary, 1913.

0448 Davison, William T. *The Indwelling Spirit.* Hodder & Stoughton, 1911.

0449 Dawe, Donald G. "Divinity of the Holy Spirit," *Int* 33 (January 1979): 19–31.

0450 Dawson, Ernest. *Spiritual Religion.* Longmans, Green & Co., 1914.

0451 Dayton, Donald W. "Doctrine of the Baptism of the Holy Spirit: Its Emergence and Significance," *WTJ* 13 (Spring 1978): 114–26.

0452 ______. "From Christian Perfection to the 'Baptism of the Holy Ghost,'" in *Aspects of Pentecostal-Charismatic Origins,* Vinson Synan, editor. Logos International, 1975. Pp. 39–54.

0453 ______. *Late Nineteenth Century Revivalist Teachings on the Holy Spirit.* Garland Publishing, 1985.

0454 ______. "Theological Roots of Pentecostalism," *P* 2:1 (Spring 1980): 3–21.

0455 De Zordi, Gianni. "L'esperienza liturgica dello spirto." Unpublished dissertation, Pontificia Universitas, 1977.

0456 Dean, Bryant Edward. "The Holy Spirit and Human Leadership." Unpublished dissertation, New Orleans Baptist Seminary, 1972.

0457 Dearmer, Percy. *The Power of the Spirit.* Oxford University Press, 1919.

0458 Deasley, Alex R. G. "Entire Sanctification and the Baptism with the Holy Spirit: Perspectives on the Biblical View of the Relationship," *WTJ* 14 (Spring 1979): 27–44.

0459 DeHaan, M. R. *Holy Spirit Baptism.* Radio Bible Class, 1964.

0460 Delarue, Jacques. *A la rencontre de l'Esprit Saint.* Les Editions du Cerf, 1978.

0461 Delgado, Varela Jose M. "Renovacion Carismatica Catolica en Guatemala," *EsTe* 2 (July-December 1975): 227–60.

0462 Demaray, Donald E. "The Spirit-Filled Life," in *Insights into Holiness,* Kenneth Geiger, editor. Beacon Hill Press, 1962. Pp. 209–22.

0463 Denham, William Ernest. *The Comforter: A Brief Discussion of the Person and Work of the Holy Spirit.* Revell Co., 1935.

0464 Denlo, Francis B. *The Supreme Leader: A Study of the Nature and Work of the Holy Spirit.* Pilgrim Press, 1900.

0465 DeRosa, Peter. *Come Holy Spirit: The Life of God in the Life of Men.* Collins, 1975.

0466 Derrett, J. Duncan M. "Simon Magus (Acts 8:9–24)," *ZNW* 73:1–2 (1982): 52–68.

0467 Deterding, Paul E. "Baptism According to the Apostle Paul," *ConJ* 6:3 (May 1980): 93–100.

0468 Detweiler, Richard C. "The Incarnational Work of the Holy Spirit," in *Encounter with the Holy Spirit,* George R. Brunk, II, editor. Herald Press, 1972. Pp. 210–20.

0469 Devenny, Thomas A. "The Holy Spirit as the Interpreter of the Old Testament in the New Testament Community." Unpublished dissertation, Southern Baptist Seminary, 1961.

0470 Dewar, Daniel. *The Holy Spirit: His Personality, Divinity, Office, and Agency.* Ward & Company, 1847.

0471 Dewar, Lindsay. *The Holy Spirit and Modern Thought.* Harper & Brothers, 1959.

0472 Di Gangi, Mariano. *The Spirit of Christ.* Baker Book House, 1975.

0473 Dierks, Friedrich Adolf Johannes. "The Cross-Cultural Communication of the Christian Message: Aspects of the Christian Proclamation Among the Tswana." Unpublished dissertation, University of South Africa, 1982.

0474 Dillenschneider, Clément. *The Holy Spirit and the Priest.* Herder, 1965.

0475 Dillistone, Frederick W. "The Biblical Doctrine of the Holy Spirit," *ThTo* 3 (January 1947): 486–97.

0476 ______. *The Holy Spirit in the Life of Today.* Westminster Press, 1947.

0477 Dilschneider, Otto. *Gegenwart Christi.* C. Bertelsmann, 1948.

0478 ______. *Ich Glaube an den Heiligen Geist.* R. Brockhaus, 1969.

0479 Ditmanson, Harold H. "The Significance of the Doctrine of the Holy Spirit for Contemporary Theology," in *The Holy Spirit in the Life of the Church: From Biblical Times to the Present,* Paul D. Opsahl, editor. Augsburg Publishing Co., 1978. Pp. 204–20.

0480 Dixon, Amzi C., ed. *The Holy Spirit in Life and Service: Addresses Delivered Before the Conference on the Ministry of the Holy Spirit.* Revell Co., 1895.

0481 ______. *The Person and the Ministry of the Holy Spirit.* Wharton, Barron & Company, 1890.

0482 Dixon, Philip J. "Social Aspects of the Holy Spirit as Foundation for Church Empowerment." Unpublished dissertation, Wesley Seminary, 1974.

0483 Dockx, S. "L'Eglise, épiphanie de l'Esprit Saint," in *L'Esprit Saint et L'Eglise.* Fayard, 1969. Pp. 235–58.

0484 Dominy, Bert. "Paul and Spiritual Gifts: Reflections on 1 Corinthians 12–14," *SWJT* 26:1 (Fall 1983): 49–68.

0485 Donne, Brian K. "Significance of the Ascension of Jesus Christ in the New Testament," *SJT* 30:6 (1977): 555–68.

0486 Dooley, Lester M. *Further Discourses on the Holy Ghost.* Frederick Pustet Co., Inc., 1945.

0487 Dörries, Hermann. *De Spiritu Sancto.* Vandenhoeck & Ruprecht, 1956.

0488 Doty, Thomas K. *The Two-Fold Gift of the Holy Ghost.* T. B. Arnold, 1901.

0489 Doty, Walter M. "The Holy Spirit—Biblical Backgrounds," in *Dynamics of the Faith,* Gene Miller, Max Gaulke, Donald Smith, editors. Gulf-Coast Bible College, 1972. Pp. 162–80.

0490 Douglas, James D. *Let the Earth Hear His Voice: International Congress on World Evangelization, Lausanne, Switzerland: Official Reference Volume (1974).* World Wide Publishers, 1975.

0491 Dowden, Milton L. "Why Did Paul Rebaptize the Twelve Disciples in Acts 19:1–7." Unpublished report, Grace Seminary, 1950.

0492 Downer, Arthur C. *The Mission and Ministration of the Holy Spirit.* T. & T. Clark, 1909.

0493 Dragas, George D. "Holy Spirit and Tradition: The Writings of St. Athanasius," *Sob* NS 1:1 (1979): 51–72.

0494 Drake, Frederick W. *The Spirit of Glory.* Longmans, Green & Co., 1927.

0495 Dreyfus, F. "L'Actualisation de l'Ecriture: Du Texte à la vie; L'Action de L'Esprit: La Place de la Tradition" (part 1), *RBib* 86 (January 1979): 5–58.

0496 ______. "L'Actualisation de l'Ecriture: Du Texte à la vie; L'Action de L'Esprit: La Place de la Tradition" (part 2), *RBib* 86 (April 1979): 161–93.

0497 ______. "L'Actualisation de l'Ecriture: Du Texte à la vie; L'Action de L'Esprit: La Place de la Tradition" (part 3), *RBib* (July 1979): 321–93.

0498 Driver, George H. *What Has Become of the Doctrine of the Holy Spirit?* Hicks-Gaston Company, 1936.

0499 Drummond, Lewis A. *Life Can Be Real.* Lakeland, 1973.

0500 Dubarle, A. M. "L'Esprit Saint et la liturgie d'après l'Ecriture Sainte," in *Le Saint-Esprit dans la Liturgie,* A. Pistoia and A. Triacca, editors. Bibliotheca Ephemerides Liturgicae, 1977. Pp. 71–86.

0501 Dubay, Thomas. "Ministerial Leadership and Discernment," *Com* 3 (Spring 1976): 50–66.

0502 Ducharme, Alfred. *Spiritual Discernment and Community Deliberation.* Canadian Religious Conference, 1974.

0503 Duewel, Wesley L. *The Holy Spirit and Tongues.* Light and Life Press, 1974.

0504 Dufort, Jean M. "Comportements et Attitudes dans les Groupes Charismatiques: Une Lecture Herméneutique," *SEs* 30 (October-December): 255–78.

0505 ______. "Vues Prospectives sur le Renouveau Charismatique dans les Eglises Chrétiennes," *SEs* 31 (January-April 1979): 61–79.

0506 Dukkeit, Gerhard. *Die Idee Gottes im Geiste der Philosophie Hegels.* Herman Rinn, 1947.

0507 Dumais, Marcel "Ministères, Charismes et Esprit dans l'Oeuvre de Luc," *EgTh* 9 (October 1978): 413–53.

0508 Duncan, George B. *The Renewing Spirit: The Person and Work of the Holy Spirit in the Life of the Believer.* John Knox Press, 1975.

0509 Dunne, Tad. "Trinity and History," *ThSt* 45 (March 1984): 139–52.

0510 Dunn, James D. G. *Baptism in the Holy Spirit: A Re-Examination of the New Testament Teaching on the Gift of the Spirit in Relation to Pentecostalism Today.* SCM Press, 1970.

0511 ______. "Birth of a Metaphor: Baptized in the Spirit" (part 1), *ExT* 89:5 (1978): 134–38.

0512 ______. "Birth of a Metaphor: Baptized in the Spirit" (part 2), *ExT* 89:6 (1978): 173–75.

0513 ______. "1 Corinthians 15:45: Last Adam, Life-Giving Spirit," in *Christ and Spirit in the New Testament: Essays in Honour of Charles Francis Digby Moule,* Barnabas Lindars et al., editors. Cambridge University Press, 1973. Pp. 127–41.

0514 ______. "Discernment of Spirits—a Neglected Gift," in *Witness to the Spirit: Essays on Revelation, Spirit, Redemption,* Wilfrid Harrington, editor. Koinonia Press, 1979. Pp. 79–96.

0515 ______. *Jesus and the Spirit.* SCM Press, 1975.

0516 ______. "Rediscovering the Spirit," *ExT* 84 (1972): 7–12, 40–44.

0517 ______. "Romans 7:14–25 in the Theology of Paul," in *Essays on Apostolic Themes: Studies in Honor of Howard M. Ervin.* Paul Elbert, editor. Hendrickson Publishers, 1985. Pp. 49–70.

0518 ______. "Spirit-and-Fire Baptism," *NT* 14 (1972): 81–92.

0519 ______. "Spirit-Baptism and Pentecostalism," *SJT* 23 (1970): 397–407.

0520 Dunn, Lewis R. *The Mission of the Spirit.* Carlton & Lanaham, 1872.

0521 Du Plessis, David. "Holy Spirit in Ecumenical Movement," in *Jesus, Where are You Taking Us? Messages from the First International Lutheran Conference on the Holy Spirit.* Creation House, 1973. Pp. 223–50.

0522 ______. *The Spirit Bade Me Go.* Privately published, 1963.

0523 Du Pleiss, J. G. "The Fruit of the Spirit in the Life of the Individual and Society," in *The Spirit in Biblical Perspective,* W. S. Vorster, editor. University of South Africa, 1980. Pp. 66–79.

0524 DuPont, Jacques. "Le Prière et son Efficacité dans L'Evangile de luc," *ReSR* 69 (January-March 1981): 45–55.

0525 Dupuy, B.-D. "Esprit saint et anthropologie chrétienne," in *L'Esprit Saint et L'Eglise.* Fayard, 1969. Pp. 307–26.

0526 Duquoc, Christian. "Charism as the Social Expression of the Unpredictable Nature of Grace," in *Charisms in the Church,* Christian Duquoc and Casiano Floristan, editors. Seabury Press, 1978. Pp. 87–96.

0527 Durand, Guy M. "Un Passage du 3E Livre Contre Eunome de s Basile dans la Tradition Manucrite," *Iren* 54:1 (1981): 36–52.

0528 Durand, J. A., et al., eds. *Studies in the Johannine Letters (Proceedings of 15th Meeting of New Testament Society of South Africa, 1979).* New Testament Society of South Africa, 1981.

0529 Durken, Daniel. *Sin, Salvation and the Spirit.* Liturgical Press, 1979.

0530 DuToit, Barend Abraham. "The Receipt of the Holy Spirit in Samaria: An Exegetical Study of Acts 8:14–17." Unpublished dissertation, University of South Africa, 1978.

0531 Dyches, John W. "Biblical Worship: Its Spirit and Teaching." Unpublished dissertation, Southern Baptist Seminary, 1900.

E

0532 Easley, Kendell H. "The Pauline Usage of *Pneumati* as a Reference to the Spirit of God," *JETS* 27 (1984): 299–313.

0533 Ebhomielen, Paul Omieka. "Gustaf Aulen's Christus Victor View of Atonement as it Relates to the Demonic in Africa." Unpublished dissertation, Baylor University, 1982.

0534 Eckle, Wolfgang. *Geist und Logos bei Cicero und im Johannesevangelium.* Georg Olms, 1978.

0535 Edel, Reiner-Friedemann. *Im Fraftfeld des Heiligen Geistes.* Edel, 1968.

0536 ———. *Kirche und Charisma. Die Gaben des Heiligen Geistes im Neuen Testament, in der Kirchengeschichte und in der Gegenwart.* Edel, 1966.

0537 Edsman, Carl-Martin. *Le Baptême de feu.* Alfred Lorentz, 1940.

0538 Edwards, James F. *The Holy Spirit: The Christian Dynamic.* Christian Literature Society for India, 1918.

0539 Edwards, Jonathan, revised by T. O. Summers. *The Work of the Holy Spirit in the Human Heart.* Publishing House of M. E. Church, South, 1903.

0540 Egert, Eugene. *The Holy Spirit in German Literature Until the End of the Twelfth Century.* Mouton, 1973.

0541 von Eicken, Erich. *Heiliger Geist, Menschengeist, Schwarmgeist. Ein Beitrag zur Geschichte der Pfingstbewegung in Deutschland.* R. Brockhaus, 1964.

0542 Eklund, Ryan Bellman, Jr. "A Biblical Study of the Spirit of God in Isaiah." Unpublished dissertation, Southern Baptist Seminary, 1957.

0543 Elbert, Paul. "Calvin and the Spiritual Gifts," in *Essays on Apostolic Themes: Studies in Honor of Howard M. Ervin.* Paul Elbert, editor. Hendrickson Publishers, 1985. Pp. 115–43.

0544 ______. "Calvin and the Spiritual Gifts," *JETS* 22 (September 1979): 235–56.

0545 Eliot, William G. *The Holy Spirit.* Unitarian Society for the Diffusion of Knowledge, 1866.

0546 Ellis, E. Earle. " 'Spiritual Gifts' in the Pauline Community," *NTS* 10 (1974): 128–44.

0547 Elmer, Walter D. "A Study of the Doctrine of the Holy Spirit in the Old Testament Religious Experience." Unpublished thesis, Western Evangelical Seminary, 1950.

0548 Emilianos of Silibria. "The Triune God in the Life-Giving Process," in *Jesus Christ: The Life of the World,* Ion Bria, editor. World Council of Churches, 1982. Pp. 64–72.

0549 Enang, K. N. "The Holy Spirit in the Nigerian Independent Churches," *SAM* 9:2 (1976): 3–31.

0550 Engel, Frank G., et al., eds. *Authorities in Moral Behaviour: 6th Meeting of Joint Working Group of Australian Council of Churches and Roman Catholic Church, Sydney.* Australian Council of Churches, 1972.

0551 Engelbrecht, Ben. "The Indwelling of the Holy Spirit, Part 1: An Evaluation of Contemporary Pneumatology," *JTSA* 30 (March 1980): 19–33.

0552 ______. "The Indwelling of the Holy Spirit, Part 2: A Contemporary Statement," *JTSA* 31 (June 1980): 36–45.

0553 Englezakis, Benedict. "Should the Orthodox Speak of a 'Temporal Procession' of the Holy Spirit," *EChR* 9:1 (1977): 91–94.

0554 Eno, Robert B. "Pope and Council: The Patristic Origins," *SEs* 28 (May-September 1976): 183–211.

0555 Erdman, Charles R. *The Spirit of Christ.* R. R. Smith, 1929.

0556 Erhueh, Anthony Ojagberovwe. "The Image of God in Man in Vatican II: An Inquiry into the Theological Foundations and Significance of Human Dignity in the Pastoral Constitution on the Church in the Modern World." Unpublished dissertation, Fordham University, 1982.

0557 Erickson, Craig Douglas. "Sacramental Theology Among American Presbyterians: 1945–1979." Unpublished dissertation, University of Notre Dame, 1982.

0558 Erni, Raymund. "Pneumatologische und Triadologische Ekklesiologie in ihrer Bedeutung für Struktur und Leben der Kirche: ein Beitrag aus der Sicht," in *Unterwegs zur Einheit,* Johannes Brantschen and Pietro Selvatico, editors. Herder, 1980. Pp. 803–20.

0559 Ervin, Howard M. *Conversion-Initiation and the Baptism in the Holy Spirit.* Hendrickson Publishers, 1986.

0560 ______. "Hermeneutics: A Pentecostal Option," *P* 3:2 (Fall 1981): 11–25.

0561 ______. "Hermeneutics: A Pentecostal Option," in *Essays on Apostolic Themes: Studies in Honor of Howard M. Ervin.* Paul Elbert, editor. Hendrickson Publishers, 1985. Pp. 23–35.

0562 ______. *Spirit Baptism: A Biblical Investigation.* Hendrickson Publishers, 1987.

0563 ______. *These Are Not Drunken as Ye Suppose.* Logos International, 1968.

0564 Esquerda, Bifet Juan. "El Apostol Testigo Y Cooperador de la Accion del Espiritu Santo en el Mundo," *EsTe* 4 (January-July 1977): 215–24.

0565 ______. "Espiritualidad Mariana Como Fidelidad a la Mision del Espiritu Santo," *EsTe* 2 (July-December 1975): 155–67.

0566 Estes, J. R. "A Biblical Concept of Spiritual Gifts." Unpublished dissertation, Southern Baptist Seminary, 1957.

0567 Etienne, Anne. "Etude du Récit de l'Evénement de Pentecôte dans Actes 2," *FV* 80 (January 1981): 47–67.

0568 ______. "Profils de l'Esprit et Evénment de Pentecôte," *FV* 80 (January 1981): 1–122.

0569 Ettlinger, Gerard H. "The Holy Spirit in the Theology of the Second Ecumenical Synod and in the Undivided Church," *GOTR* 27 (Winter 1982): 431–40.

0570 Evans, Louis Hadley. *Life's Hidden Power: The Gift of the Spirit.* Revell Co., 1959.

0571 Evans, Owen E. "Except by the Holy Spirit (Sermon, Whitsunday: 1 Corinthians 12:3)," *ExT* 70 (April 1959): 222–24.

0572 ______. "New Wine in Old Wineskins: XIII," *ExT* 86 (April 1975): 196–200.

0573 Evans, Robert A. and Thomas D. Parker. *Christian Theology: A Case Method Approach.* Harper and Row, 1976.

0574 Evdokimoff, Paul. *L'Esprit Saint dans la Tradition Orthodoxe.* Les Editions du Cerf, 1969.

0575 ______. "L'Esprit saint et l'Eglise, d'après la tradition liturgique," in *L'Esprit Saint et L'Eglise.* Fayard, 1969. Pp. 85–111.

0576 Every, Edward. "The Filioque Question (Jn 15:26)," *Sob* NS 1:2 (1979): 42–49.

0577 ______. "Proceeding from the Father to the Son," *EChR* 10:1–2 (1978): 145–47.

0578 Ewer, Ferdinand Cartwright. *Four Confessions Touching the Operation of the Holy Spirit.* G. P. Putnams, 1880.

0579 Ewert, David. "The Baptizing Work of the Holy Spirit," in *Encounter with the Holy Spirit,* George R. Brunk, II, editor. Herald Press, 1972. Pp. 26–45.

0580 ______. "Born of the Spirit," in *Encounter with the Holy Spirit,* George R. Brunk, II, editor. Herald Press, 1972. Pp. 16–25.

0581 ______. "Glossolalia in the Church Today," in *Encounter with the Holy Spirit,* George R. Brunk, II, editor. Herald Press, 1972. Pp. 174–88.

0582 ______. *The Holy Spirit in the New Testament.* Herald Press, 1983.

F

0583 Faber, George S. *A Practical Treatise on the Ordinary Operations of the Holy Spirit.* N.p., n.d.

0584 Faber, Heije. *De leer van de heiligen Geest: Studie over eenige actueele vraagstukken der moderne theologie.* Van Loghum Slaterus, 1941.

0585 Fahey, Michael. "Son and Spirit: Divergent Theologies between Constantinople and the West," in *Conflicts about the Holy Spirit,* Hans Küng and Jürgen Moltmann, editors. Seabury Press, 1979. Pp. 15–22.

0586 Faricy, Robert. "Nature, Social Sin, and the Spirit," in *The Spirit of God in Christian Life,* Edward Malatesta, editor. Paulist Press, 1977. Pp. 75–97.

0587 Farina, John Edward. "Isaac Hecker and the Holy Spirit." Unpublished dissertation, Columbia University, 1979.

0588 Farnsworth, Kirk E., Joseph M. Alexanian, and Jerome D. Iverson. "Integration and the Culture of Rationalism: Reaction to Responses to 'The Conduct of Integration,' " *JPTh* 11 (Winter 1983): 349–52.

0589 Fatula, Mary Ann. "The Council of Florence and Pluralism in Dogma," *OC* 19:1 (1983): 14–27.

0590 ______. "The Holy Spirit and Human Actualization Through Love: Contribution of Aquinas," *TD* 32:2 (1985): 217–24.

0591 ______. "The Holy Spirit in East and West: Two Irreducible Traditions," *OC* 19:4 (1983): 379–86.

0592 ______. "A Problematic Western Formula (Tamquam ab uno Principio)," *OC* 17:4 (1981): 324–34.

0593 Fedwick, Paul J. *Basil of Caesarea: Christian Humanist, Ascetic.* 2 vols. Pontifical Institute of Medieval Studies, 1981.

0594 *Fellowship of the Holy Spirit: Eight Bible Studies.* World Council of Churches, 1970.

0595 Ferguson, John. "Whitsunday: The Holy Spirit (Acts 19:1–2; Sermon)," *ExT* 94 (May 1983): 240–42.

0596 Festugiere, A. J. "Le Voile de l'Epiclese," *RHR* 186 (July 1974): 45–53.

0597 Fiala, Virgil. "L'imposition des mains comme signe de la communication de l'Esprit Saint dans les rites latins," in *Le Saint-Esprit dans la Liturgie,* A. Pistoia and A. Triacca, editors. Bibliotheca Ephemerides Liturgicae, 1977. Pp. 87–103.

0598 Fieck, Lerome L. "The Doctrine of the Holy Spirit in Contemporary Thought," *BETS* 3:3 (Summer 1960).

0599 Fife, Eric S. *The Holy Spirit: Common Sense and the Bible.* Zondervan, 1978.

0600 Fine, Lawrence Brian. "Techniques of Mystical Meditation for Achieving Prophecy and the Holy Spirit in the Teachings of Isaac Luria and Hayyim Vital." Unpublished dissertation, Brandeis University, 1976.

0601 Fink, Peter E. "The Sacrament of Orders: Some Liturgical Reflections," *Wor* 56 (November 1982): 482–502.

0602 Finley, Clyde Stephen. "Ruskin's Evangelical Covenant with Nature." Unpublished dissertation, University of Virginia, 1982.

0603 Firor, W. M. "Fulfillment of the Promise: The Holy Spirit and the Christian Life," *Int* 7 (1953): 299–314.

0604 Fischer, B. "The Meaning of the Expression 'Baptism of the Spirit' in the Light of Catholic Baptismal Liturgy and Spirituality," *OC* 10 (1974): 172–73.

0605 Fischer-Wollpert, Rudolf. *Der Schöpfer Geist.* Winfried-Werk, 1966.

0606 Fison, Joseph Edward. *The Blessing of the Holy Spirit.* Longmans, Green & Co., 1950.

0607 ______. *Fire Upon the Earth.* Edinburg House Press, 1958.

0608 Fitch, William. Ministry of the Holy Spirit. Zondervan, 1974.

0609 Fletcher, John. *The Works of the Reverend John Fletcher.* 4 vols. Lane and Scott, 1851.

0610 Flew, R. Newton. *The Idea of Perfection in Christian Theology.* Oxford University Press, 1934.

0611 Floristan, Casiano and Christian Duquoc. *Learning to Pray.* Seabury Press, 1982.

0612 Foerster W. "Der Heilige Geist im sog. Spätjudentum," in *De Spiritu Sancto.* Kemick, 1964. Pp. 40–62.

0613 Fokkema, Fokke Jansz. *Ik geloof in den Heiligen Geist.* Zendingsbureau, 1927.

0614 Folkemer, Lawrence D. "Dialogue and Proclamation," *JES* 13 (Summer 1976): 420–39.

0615 Folsom, John Dana. *The Holy Spirit Our Helper.* The Methodist Book Concern, 1907.

0616 Ford, Francis X. *Come, Holy Spirit: Thoughts on Renewing the Earth as the Kingdom of God.* Orbis Books, 1976.

0617 Ford, J. Massyngberde. *Baptism of the Spirit: Three Essays on the Pentecostal Experience.* Divine Word Publications, 1971.

0618 ______. *Ministries and Fruits of the Holy Spirit.* Catholic Action Office, 1973.

0619 ______. *The Spirit and the Human Person: A Meditation.* Pflaum Press, 1969.

0620 Fortman, Edmund J. *Activities of the Holy Spirit.* Franciscan Herald Press, 1984.

0621 Foster, John. "The Gift of the Holy Spirit (Sermon, Whitsunday: Acts 2:39)," *ExT* 62 (1951): 215–17.

0622 Fourman, Larry David. "The Holy Spirit in the New Testament: Directors for Renewing the Local Congregation." Unpublished dissertation, Bethany Theological Seminary, 1979.

0623 Fraikin, Daniel. " 'Charismes et Ministères': A la Lumière de 1 Cor 12–14," *EgTh* 9 (October 1978): 455–63.

0624 Frazier, Claude A. *Healing and Religious Faith.* Pilgrim Press, 1974.

0625 Freeman, Clifford Wade. *The Holy Spirit's Ministry.* Zondervan, 1954.

0626 Freeman, D. "Feast of Pentecost," in *The New Bible Dictionary,* J. D. Douglas, editor. Eerdmans Publishing Co., 1962. P. 731.

0627 Frey, Christofer. "Kriterien der Gegenwart des Heiligen Geistes," in *Das Religiöse Bewusstsein und der Heilige Geist in der Kirche,* Klaus Kremkau, editor. Otto Lembeck, 1980. Pp. 53–73.

0628 Frey, William. "The Spirit and Community," in *Bishop's Move,* Michael Harper, editor. Hodder & Stoughton, 1978. Pp. 77–100.

0629 Freyer, Thomas. *Pneumatologie als Strukturprinzip der Dogmatik.* Schöningh, 1982.

0630 Friedel, Henri. "Visages de la 'Demesure,'" *ETR* 52:4 (1977): 509–18.

0631 Friedenshort, Sister Eva of. *The Working of the Holy Spirit in Daily Life.* Hughs Press, 1949.

0632 Fritzsche, Helmut. "Der Christliche Gott als der Trinitarische Gott (Vortag, 20ten Konferenz der Hochschultheologen der Ostseeländer, Turku, Juni 1981)," *ThLit* 107 (January 1982): 2–12.

0633 Frodsham, Stanley. *Smith Wigglesworth: Apostle of Faith.* Gospel Publishing House, 1949.

0634 Froelich, Karlfried. "Charismatic Manifestations and the Lutheran Incarnational Stance," in *The Holy Spirit in the Life of the Church: From Biblical Times to the Present,* Paul D. Opsahl, editor. Augsburg Publishing Co., 1978. Pp. 136–57.

0635 Frøen, Hans J. "What is Baptism in the Holy Spirit?" in *Jesus, Where are You Taking Us? Messages from the First International Lutheran Conference on the Holy Spirit,* Norris L. Wogen, editor. Creation House, 1973. Pp. 113–32.

0636 Froget, Barthelemy. *The Indwelling of the Holy Spirit in the Souls of the Just according to the Teaching of St. Thomas Aquinas.* Paulist Press, 1921.

0637 Frost, Henry W. *Who Is the Holy Spirit?* Revell Co., 1938.

0638 Frost, Robert C. *Aglow with the Spirit.* Voice Christian Publications, 1965.

0639 ______. *Biology of the Holy Spirit.* Revell Co., 1975.

0640 ______. *Overflowing Life.* Logos International, 1971.

0641 ______. *Set My Spirit Free.* Logos International, 1973.

0642 Fuchs, Ernst. "Der Anteil des Paulus: Ein Beitrag zum Verständnis von Römer 8," *ZTK* 72:3 (1975): 293–302.

0643 Fuller, Reginald H. "Tongues in the New Testament," *ACQ* 3 (Fall 1963): 162–68.

0644 Fung, Ronald Y. K. "Ministry, Community and Spiritual Gifts (in Pauline Theology)," *EQ* 56 (January 1984): 3–20.

0645 ______. "Some Pauline Pictures of the Church (Reply, D. Denton, 54, 147–49 Jl-S 82)," *EQ* 53 (April-June 1981): 89–107.

G

0646 Gabelein, A. C. *The Holy Spirit in the New Testament.* Our Hope, n.d.

0647 Gaffin, Richard B. "The Holy Spirit," *WTJ* 43 (Fall 1980): 58–78.

0648 ______. "Old Amsterdam and Inerrancy (The Writings of Abraham Kuyper and Herman Bavinck on the Doctrine of Scripture; Part 1)," *WTJ* 44:2 (Fall 1982): 250–89.

0649 ______. *Perspectives on Pentecost: Studies in New Testament Teaching on the Gifts of the Holy Spirit.* Presbyterian and Reformed Publishing Company, 1979.

0650 Gallaway, Ira. *Drifted Astray: Returning the Church to Witness and Ministry.* Abingdon Press, 1983.

0651 Galloway, Allan D. "Recent Thinking on Christian Beliefs, III: The Holy Spirit in Recent Theology," *ExT* 88 (January 1977): 100–103.

0652 Galtier, Paul. *Le Saint Esprit en nous d'après les pères grecs.* Pontifical Universitatis, 1946.

0653 Gangel, Kenneth O. *You and Your Spiritual Gifts.* Moody Press, 1975.

0654 Ganoczy, Alexandre. "Formale und inhaltiche Aspekte der Mittelalterlichen Konzilien als Zeichen Kirchlichen Ringens um ein Universales Glaubensbekenntnis," in *Glaubensbekenntnis und Kirchengemeinschaft,* K. Lehmann, editor. Herder, 1982. Pp. 49–79.

0655 ______. "Word and Spirit in Catholic Tradition," in *Conflicts about the Holy Spirit,* Hans Küng and Jürgen Moltmann, editors. Seabury Press, 1979. Pp. 48–59.

0656 Garcia, Moreno Antonio. "La Realesa Y el Senorio de Cristo en Tcsaloniccnscs," *EB* Ns 39:1 2 (1981): 63–82.

0657 Gardeil, Ambroise. *The Holy Spirit in the Christian Life.* Blackfriars Publications, 1953.

0658 Gardiner, F. *The Power of the Spirit.* Scribner's, 1920.

0659 Garrett, D. D. "The Holy Spirit and Our Lay Ministry," *AZQR* 93:3 (October 1981): 42–43.

0660 Garrett, James. "Biblical Authority According to Baptist Confessions of Faith," *RE* 76 (Winter 1979): 43–54.

0661 Garrison, James Harvey. *The Holy Spirit: His Personality, Mission and Modes of Activity.* Christian Publishing Company, 1905.

0662 Garvie, Alfred E. *The Purpose of God in Christ and Its Fulfillment Through the Holy Spirit.* Hodder & Stoughton, 1918.

0663 Gasparro, Giulia S. "Personaggio di Sophia Nel Vangelo Secondo Filippo," *VigChr* 31:4 (1977): 244–81.

0664 Gealy, Fred Daniel. "The Significance of Jesus for the Holy Spirit Experiences in the Pre-Pauline Church." Unpublished dissertation, Boston University Graduate School, 1929.

0665 Geanakoplos, Deno J. "The Second Ecumenical Synod of Constantinople (381): Proceedings and Theology of the Holy Spirit," *GOTR* 27 (Winter 1982): 407–29.

0666 Gearhart, Joseph E. *What Jesus Said About the Holy Ghost.* Christian Standard Company, 1903.

0667 Gee, Donald. *Fruitful or Barren: Studies in the Fruit of the Spirit.* Gospel Publishing House, 1961.

0668 ______. *God's Great Gift.* Gospel Publishing House, n.d.

0669 ______. "The Initial Evidence of the Baptism of the Holy Spirit," *RéT* 45 (1959): 10–12.

0670 ______. *Keeping in Touch: Studies on "Walking in the Spirit."* Elim Publishing Company, 1951.

0671 ______. *The Ministry Gifts of Christ.* Gospel Publishing House, 1930.

0672 Geense, Adriaan. "Pneumatologische Entwürfe in der Niederländischen Theologie," *ThLit* 106 (November 1981): 785–96.

0673 Geiger, Kenneth, et al., eds. "Studies in Contemporary Wesleyan-Arminian Theology," in *The Word and the Doctrine,* Kenneth E. Geiger, editor. Beacon Hill Press, 1965. N.p.

0674 Gelpi, Donald L. "Conversion: The Challenge of Contemporary Charismatic Piety," *ThSt* 43 (December 1982): 606–28.

0675 ______. *The Divine Mother: A Trinitarian Theology of the Holy Spirit.* University Press of America, 1984.

0676 ______. "Ecumenical Reflections on Christ's Eucharistic Presence," in *Essays on Apostolic Themes: Studies in Honor of Howard M. Ervin.* Paul Elbert, editor. Hendrickson Publishers, 1985. Pp. 193–20.

0677 ______. *Experiencing God: A Theology of Human Experience.* Paulist Press, 1978.

0678 George, A. Raymond. "L'Esprit Saint dans L'Oeuvre de Luc," *RBib* 85 (October 1978): 500–542.

0679 ______. "The Holy Spirit Transforms the Human Community into the Kingdom of God," *OC* 16:3 (1980): 214–24.

0680 Gerig Jared F. "The Gifts of the Spirit," in *Insights into Holiness,* Kenneth Geiger, editor. Beacon Hill Press, 1962. Pp. 241–62.

0681 Gero, Stephen. "Spirit as a Dove at the Baptism of Jesus," *NT* 18 (January 1976): 71–75.

0682 Gerrard, William Austin, III. "Walter Scott: Frontier Disciples Evangelist." Unpublished dissertation, Emory University, 1982.

0683 Geyer, G. Robert. *Empowerment of the Laity with the Charismata for Renewal in a Traditional Congregation.* Rochester: Colgate, 1983.

0684 Giblet, C. J. "Baptism in the Spirit in the Acts of the Apostles," *OC* 10 (1974): 162–71.

0685 Gickler, Dominikus M. *Weltmission im heiligen Geist.* N.p., 1955.

0686 Gilbert, Arthur. "Pentecost Among the Pentecostals," *CC* 78 (June 28, 1961): 794–96.

0687 Gilbert, Marvin G. and Raymond T. Brock, ed. *The Holy Spirit and Counseling.* Hendrickson Publishers, 1986.

0688 Giles, Kevin N. "Present-Future Eschatology in the Book of Acts" (part 1), *RefThR* 40 (September-December 1981): 65–71.

0689 ______. "Present-Future Eschatology in the Book of Acts" (part 2), *RefThR* 41 (January-April 1982): 11–18.

0690 Gilfillan, Samuel. *Practical Views of the Dignity, Grace, and Operations of the Holy Spirit.* William Oliphant, 1826.

0691 Gilkey, Langdon. "The Spirit and the Discovery of the Truth through Dialogue," in *Experience of the Spirit,* Peter Huizing and William Bassett. Seabury Press, 1974. Pp. 58–68.

0692 Gillespie, James T. "The Work of the Holy Spirit as Shown in the Book of Acts." Unpublished dissertation, Southern Baptist Seminary, 1930.

0693 Gillespie, Thomas. "Prophecy and Tongues: The Concept of Christian Prophecy in the Pauline Theology." Unpublished dissertation, Claremont Graduate School, 1971.

0694 Gillièron, Bernard. *Le Saint-Esprit.* Labor et Fides, 1978.

0695 Gillquist, Peter E. *Let's Quit Fighting about the Holy Spirit.* Zondervan, 1974.

0696 Gils, Félix. *Désaltères par l'unique Esprit.* Editions Saint-Paul, 1982.

0697 Girdlestone, Robert Baker. "Their Bearing on Christian Doctrine," in *Synonyms of the Old Testament.* Eerdmans Publishing Co., n.d. N.p.

0698 Gispert, Sauch George. *God's Word Among Men: Papers in Honour of Fr. Joseph Putz.* Vidajyoti Institute of Religious Studies, 1973.

0699 Glaesener, Henri. "Empereur Gratien et Saint Ambroise," *RHistE* 52 (1957): 466–88.

0700 Glardon, Christian. "Les dons spirituels dans la première épître de Paul aux Corinthiens." Unpublished thesis, Lausanne University, 1966.

0701 Glasser, Arthur F. "Report of a Happening (4th International Association for Mission Studies Conference at Maryknoll, New York, August 21–26, 1978)," *M* 7 (January 1979): 2–124.

0702 Gleason, Robert W. *The Indwelling Spirit.* Alba House, 1966.

0703 Gloël, Johannes. *Der Heilige Geist in der Heilsverkündigung des Paulus.* Max Niemeyer, 1888.

0704 "Glossolalia: 105th General Assembly of the Presbyterian Church in the United States, 1965," in *Church Studies on the Holy Spirit,* Marvin Simmers, editor. John Knox Press, 1983. Pp. 4–7.

0705 Godbey, William B. *The Incarnation of the Holy Spirit.* Pentecostal Publishing Co., n.d.

0706 ______. *Spiritual Gifts and Graces.* M. W. Knapp, 1895.

0707 ______. *Work of the Holy Spirit.* Pickett Publishing Company, 1902.

0708 Godin, André. "Moi Perdu ou Moi Retrouve dans l'Experience Charismatique: Perplexité des Psychologues," *ASSR* 20 (July-December 1975): 31–52.

0709 Goerg, Manfred. "Der Geist Gottes und der Übersetzer: Bemerkungen zu einem Brief D. Martin Luthers an Eobanus Hessus aus dem Jahre 1537," *BN* 22 (1983): 22–24.

0710 Goertz, Hans J. "Geist Und Leben: Überlegungen zur Pneumatologischen Grundlegung der Theologie," *KD* 28 (October-December 1982): 278–306.

0711 Goguel, Maurice. *La Notion johannique de l'Esprit et Ses Antécédents historiques.* Librarie Fischbacher, 1902.

0712 Goitia, José de. *La fuerza del espíritu: Pneuma-Dynamis.* Universidad de Duesto, 1974.

0713 Goldingay, John. *The Church and the Gifts of the Spirit: A Practical Exposition of 1 Corinthians 12*–14. Grove Books, 1972.

0714 Gooch, John Osborn. "The Concept of Holiness in Tertullian." Unpublished dissertation, St. Louis University, 1983.

0715 Goodman, George. *The Spirit-Led Life.* Pickering and Inglis, 1931.

0716 Goodwin, John. *Being Filled with the Spirit.* James Michael, 1867.

0717 Gordon, Adoniram Judson. *The Holy Spirit in Missions.* Revell Co., 1893.

0718 ______. *The Ministry of the Spirit.* Revell Co., 1894.

0719 Gordon, McCutchan R. C. "The Irony of Evangelical History," *JSSR* 20 (September 1981): 309–26.

0720 Gore, Charles. *The Holy Spirit and the Church.* Murray, 1924.

0721 ______. *The Reconstruction of Belief: Belief in God, Belief in Christ, the Holy Spirit and the Church.* Scribner's, 1926.

0722 Gott, Lois. "Donald Gee: The Apostle of Balance," in *Essays on Apostolic Themes: Studies in Honor of Howard M. Ervin.* Paul Elbert, editor. Hendrickson Publishers, 1985. Pp. 173–83.

0723 Gould, Marcus T. C. *A Debate between Rev. A. Campbell and Rev. N. L. Rice, on the Action, Subject, Design and Administration of Christian Baptism.* A. T. Skillman & Son, 1844.

0724 Graham, Holt H. "Gospel According to St. Mark: Mystery and Ambiguity," *ATRSS* 7 (November 1976): 43–55.

0725 Graham, William F. *The Holy Spirit.* Word Books, 1978.

0726 Grant, James. *The Comforter: The Holy Spirit in His Glorious Person and Gracious Work.* Darton and Co., 1859.

0727 Graves, Charles Lee. *The Holy Spirit in the Theology of Serguis Bulgakov.* World Council of Churches, 1972.

0728 Gray, James Martin. *The Holy Spirit in Doctrine and Life.* Revell Co., 1936.

0729 Greathouse, William. "Who Is the Holy Spirit?" in *Herald of Holiness.* Nazarene Publishing House, 1972. Pp. 8–12.

0730 Greeley, Andrew M. *The Touch of the Spirit.* Herder, 1971.

0731 Green, Michael. *I Believe in the Holy Spirit.* Eerdmans Publishing Co., 1975.

0732 Greenfield, Guy F. "The Ethical Significance of the Holy Spirit in the Writings of Paul." Unpublished dissertation, Southwestern Baptist Seminary, 1961.

0733 Greenfield, John. *Power from on High.* World Wide Revival Prayer Movement, 1931.

0734 Green, James B. *Studies in the Holy Spirit.* Revell Co., 1936.

0735 Green, Peter. *The Holy Ghost.* Longmans, Green & Co., 1933.

0736 Green, Richard. *The Works of John and Charles Wesley.* C. H. Kelly, 1896.

0737 Greet, Kenneth G. *When the Spirit Moves.* Epworth, 1975.

0738 Greeven, Heinrich. *Geistesgaben bei Paulus.* E. Gieseking, 1959.

0739 Greshman, John L., Jr. *Charles Finney's Doctrine of the Baptism of the Holy Spirit.* Hendrickson Publishers, 1987.

0740 Grewel, Hans. *Die Bedeutung des Heiligen Geistes in der Theologie Albrecht Ritschls.* Görich & Weiershäuser, 1967.

0741 Grider, J. Kenneth. "Carnality and Humanity: Exploratory Observations," *WTJ* 11 (Spring 1976): 81–91.

0742 ______. "Spirit-Baptism the Means of Sanctification: A Response to the Lyon View," *WTJ* 14 (Fall 1979): 31–50.

0743 Griffith-Thomas, W. H. *The Holy Spirit of God.* Longmans, Green & Co., 1913.

0744 Grislis, Egil. "The Challenge of the Charismatic Renewal to Lutheran Theology," *Conc* 7 (October 1981): 3–25.

0745 Grogan, Geoffrey. *What the Bible Teaches About the Holy Spirit.* Tyndale, 1979.

0746 Group of Les Dombes. "The Holy Spirit, the Church and the Sacraments," *OC* 16:3 (1980): 234–64.

0747 de Gruchy, John W. "South African Christian Leadership Assembly (SACLA) Issue," *JTSA* 29 (December 1979): 2–83.

0748 Grudem, Wayne. "Response to Gerhard Dautzenberg on 1 Corinthians 12:10," *BibZ* NS 22:2 (1978): 253–70.

0749 Grünzweig, Fritz. *Was sagt die Bibel über den Heiligen Geist?* Hänssler, 1966.

0750 Guillet, Jacques. "Baptême et Esprit," *LV* 85 (1956): 229–48.

0751 Guillet, Jacques, et al., eds. *Discernment of Spirits.* Liturgical Press, 1970.

0752 Guillou, M.-J. Le. "Réflexions sur la théologie des Pères grecs en rapport avec le *Filioque*," in *L'Esprit Saint et L'Eglise.* Fayard, 1969. Pp. 195–21.

0753 Gunkel, Hermann, with Roy A. Harrisville and Philip A. Quanbeck, II (trans.). *The Influence of the Holy Spirit: The Popular View of the Apostolic Age and the Teaching of the Apostle Paul.* Fortress Press, 1979.

0754 Gunstone, John T. A. *Live by the Spirit.* Hodder & Stoughton, 1984.

0755 Gwilym, David Vaughan. *The Spirit in the Body Mystical.* T. Whittaker, 1901.

H

0756 Haddon, A. L. "Contemporary Theology," *SQ* 10 (1949): 149–89.

0757 Haegglund, Bengt. "Die Theologie des Wortes bei Johann Gerhard," *KD* 29 (October-December 1983): 272–83.

0758 Hagin, Kenneth E. *The Holy Spirit and His Gifts.* Privately published, n.d.

0759 Haldeman, Isaac M. *Holy Ghost Baptism and Speaking with Tongues.* C. C. Cook, n.d.

0760 Haley, Emory Cleve. "Leading a Church in the Discovery and Development of the Power of the Holy Spirit in Personal and Corporate Growth." Unpublished dissertation, Southwestern Baptist Seminary, 1979.

0761 Hall, Arthur C. *The Work of the Holy Spirit.* The Young Churchman, 1907.

0762 Hall, Bert H. and Armor D. Peisker. "The Work of the Holy Spirit in Salvation," in *The Word and the Doctrine,* Kenneth E. Geiger, editor. Beacon Hill Press, 1965. Pp. 181–96.

0763 Hall, Newman. *Quench Not the Spirit.* Carter & Brothers, 1868.

0764 Hall, Robert. *Receiving the Holy Spirit.* Privately published, n.d.

0765 ______. *The Work of the Holy Spirit.* N.p., n.d.

0766 Halleux, André de. "Cyrille, Theodoret et le 'Filioque,' " *RHistE* 3–4 (1979): 597–625.

0767 ______. "Pour un Accord Oecumenique sur la Procession de l'Esprit Saint et l'Addition du 'Filioque' au Symbole," *Giren* 51:4 (1978): 451–69.

0768 Hallock, Frank H. *The Gifts of the Holy Ghost.* Morehouse Publishing Company, 1936.

0769 Hamblin, Robert Lee. *The Spirit-Filled Trauma: A Candid Plea for Biblical Understanding in the Matters of the Spirit.* Broadman Press, 1974.

0770 Hamel, Edouard. "Sexualité Illuminée par la Revelation," *StMiss* 27 (1978): 309–25.

0771 Hamer, Jerome. "Saint-Esprit et la Catholicité de l'Eglise," *AV* 46 (1969): 387–410.

0772 Hamilton, Michael P. *The Charismatic Movement.* Eerdmans Publishing Co., 1975.

0773 Hamilton, Neill Q. *The Holy Spirit and Eschatology in Paul.* Oliver and Boyd, 1957.

0774 Hammock, R. C., Jr. "A Program for Training Laypersons to Understand, Recognize, Develop, and Use the Gifts of the Holy Spirit in the Ministry of the Local Church." Unpublished dissertation, Southwestern Baptist Seminary, 1979.

0775 Hansen, Olaf. "Spirit Christology: A Way Out of Our Dilemma?" in *The Holy Spirit in the Life of the Church: From Biblical Times to the Present,* Paul D. Opsahl, editor. Augsburg Publishing Co., 1978. Pp. 172–203.

0776 Hardiment, Paschal A. "Roman Catholic-Pentecostal Dialogue: Papers from the Rome Meeting, October 1977," *OC* 19:4 (1983): 305–86.

0777 Harding, Edward. *Quench Not the Spirit.* Marshalls, 1984.

0778 Hare, Julius C. *The Mission of the Comforter.* Macmillan, 1886.

0779 Hare, Richard. "The Spirit and Worship," in *Bishop's Move,* Michael Harper, editor. Hodder & Stoughton, 1978. Pp. 121–35.

0780 Häring, Hermann. "The Role of the Spirit in the Legitimation of Ecclesial Office," in *Conflicts about the Holy Spirit,* Hans Küng and Jürgen Moltmann, editors. Seabury Press, 1979. Pp. 72–81.

0781 Harkness, Georgia Elma. *The Fellowship of the Holy Spirit.* Abingdon Press, 1966.

0782 Harkness, Henry L. and Philip Norton. *Pentecostal Praise: Consisting of One-Hundred and Eighty-Seven Hymns concerning the Holy Spirit.* Nisbet & Co., 1892.

0783 Harm, Frederick R. "A Radical Ministry of the Word and the Spirit," *ConJ* 9 (May 1983): 94–101.

0784 Harms, Paul W. *Spirit of Power.* Concordia Publishing House, 1964.

0785 Harper, Michael. *Life in the Holy Spirit: Some Questions and Answers.* Logos International, 1970.

0786 ______. *Walk in the Spirit.* Logos International, 1970.

0787 Harrington, Daniel J. "Baptism in the Holy Spirit," *CS* 11:1 (1972): 31–44.

0788 Harrington, Wilfrid. *Witness to the Spirit: Essays on Revelation, Spirit, Redemption.* Irish Biblical Association, 1979.

0789 Harrison, A. W. *John Wesley, the Last Phase.* Epworth, 1934.

0790 Harrison, Everett F. "The Holy Spirit in Acts and the Epistles," *CT* 1 (May 27, 1957): 3–4.

0791 Harrison, Michael J. "Maintenance of Enthusiasm: Involvement in a New Religious Movement," *SA* 36 (Summer 1975): 150–60.

0792 ______. "Preparation for Life in the Spirit: The Process of Initial Commitment to a Religious Movement," *ULC* 2 (1974): 387–414.

0793 Hart, Larry. "Problems of Authority in Pentecostalism," *RE* 75 (Spring 1978): 249–66.

0794 Haskins, Dan D., Jr. "Glossolalia on Campus," *Col* 8 (1978): 4.

0795 Hathaway, W. G. *Spiritual Gifts in the Church.* Elim Publishing Company, 1933.

0796 Haufe, G. "Taufe und Heiliger Geist im Urchristentum," *ThLit* 101 (1976): 562–66.

0797 Haug, Theodor. *Die Wirklichkeit des Heiligen Geistes-heute.* Vita Nova Verlag, 1947.

0798 Haughey, John C. *The Conspiracy of God: The Holy Spirit in Men.* Doubleday, 1973.

0799 Hauschild, W. D. *Gottes Geist und der Mensch.* Munich, 1972.

0800 Hawker, Robert. *Sixteen Sermons of the Divinity of Christ.* C. Routledge, 1846.

0801 Hawthorne, Gerald F. *Current Issues in Biblical and Patristic Interpretation: Studies in Honor of Merrill C. Tenney Presented by His Former Students.* Eerdmans Publishing Co., 1975.

0802 Hay, Lewis S. "Galatians 5:13 – 26," *Int* 33 (January 1979): 67 – 72.

0803 Haya-Prats, Gonzalo. *L'Esprit, force de l'Eglise: sa Nature et son activite d'après les Actes des apôtres.* Les Éditions du Cerf, 1975.

0804 Hayes, Doremus Almy. *The Gift of Tongues.* Jennings and Graham, 1913.

0805 Haykin, Michael A. G. "Makarios Silouanos: Silvanus of Tarsus and His View of the Spirit," *VigChr* 36:3 (1982): 261 – 74.

0806 ______. " 'The Spirit of God': The Exegesis of 1 Corinthians 2:10 – 12 by Origen and Athanasius," *SJT* 35:6 (1982): 513 – 28.

0807 Headlam, Arthur C. *Christian Theology: The Doctrine of God.* Clarendon Press, 1934.

0808 Hebblethwaite, Peter. "Politics of the Holy Spirit," *Front* 18 (Autumn 1975): 143 – 45.

0809 Heber, Reginald. *The Personality and Office of the Christian Comforter.* Oxford University Press, 1816.

0810 Heekeren, Henry. "Spirituality for Mission on Six Continents: Signs of the Spirit Today," *IntRMiss* 70 (October 1981): 267 – 75.

0811 Heflebower, Lori Jane. "Baptized with the Holy Spirit: Believers' Experiences in the Charismatic Movement." Unpublished dissertation, Oklahoma State University, 1982.

0812 Heimbucher, Kurt. *Das Biblische Zeugnis vom Heiligen Geist.* Gnadauer Verlag, 1973.

0813 Heitmann, Claus and Heribert Mühlen. *Erfahrung und Theologie des Heiligen Geistes.* Koesel Verlag, 1974.

0814 Heitmann, Claus and Fidelis Schmelzer. *Im Horizont des Geistes: Antwort auf Eine Krise.* Verlag Schöningh, 1971.

0815 Helandere, Jan. "Jordfastning som Mansklilgt Beteende (A Biochemical Allegory of the Body and Soul)," *SvTK* 56:1 (1980): 14 – 19.

0816 Heller, Andrew K. "Anthem Notes: Pentecost: Sundays after Pentecost," *JCM* 26:4 (April 1984): 27 – 43.

0817 Hellriegel, Martin B. "Seasonal Suggestions," *Wor* 30:6 (1956): 374 – 90.

0818 Hemke, Philip E. *Christian Stewardship Under God: Father, Son, and Holy Spirit.* Christ Seminary (Seminex), 1983.

0819 Hemphill, K. S. "The Pauline Concept of Charisma: A Situational and Developmental Approach." Unpublished dissertation, Cambridge University, 1977.

0820 Henderlite, Rachel. *The Holy Spirit in Christian Education.* Westminster Press, 1964.

0821 Henderson, Walter. "A Study of the Holy Spirit in the Farewell Discourse of Jesus." Unpublished dissertation, Western Evangelical Seminary, 1971.

0822 Hendricks, William L. "Glossolalia in the New Testament," in *Speaking in Tongues: Let's Talk About It,* Watson E. Mills, editor. Word Books, 1973. Pp. 48–60.

0823 Hendrix, Scott H. "Charismatic Renewal: Old Wine in New Skins," *CTM* 4: (June 1977): 158–66.

0824 Hendry, George S. "The Holy Spirit and the Renewal of the Church," *MTSB* (1962): 1–31.

0825 ______. *The Holy Spirit in Christian Theology.* Westminster Press, 1956.

0826 ______. *Theology of Nature.* Westminster Press, 1980.

0827 Henke, Frederick G. "Gift of Tongues and Related Phenomena at the Present Day," *AJT* 13 (April 1909): 193–206.

0828 Henry, Antonin M., with J. Lundberg and M. Bell (trans.). *The Holy Spirit.* Hawthorn Books, 1980.

0829 Henry, Paul. "Contre le Filioque," *Iren* 48:2 (1975): 170–77.

0830 Heron, Alasdair I. C. *The Holy Spirit.* Westminster Press, 1983.

0831 Herring, Ralph A. *God Being My Helper.* Broadman Press, 1955.

0832 Herrmann, Ingo. *Kyrios und Pneuma: Studien zur Christologie der Paulinischen Hauptbriefe.* Koesel Verlag, 1961.

0833 Hesselink, I. John. "Charismatic Movement and the Reformed Tradition," *RefR* 28 (Spring 1975): 147–56.

0834 Heufelder, Emmanuel M. " 'Gemeinschaft des Heiligen Geistes' 2 Kor 13:13," in *Ich Glaube Eine Heilige Kirche: H. Asmussen,* Walter Bauer, et al., editors. Evangelisches Verlag, 1963. Pp. 41–46.

0835 Hewlett, I. *Thoughts on the Holy Spirit and His Work.* J. Snow, 1845.

0836 Heyer, Robert. *Scripture and the Church.* Paulist Press, 1976.

0837 Hill, D. *New Testament Prophecy.* Marshall, Morgan & Scott, 1979.

0838 Hinchcliff, John, Jack Lewis, and Kapil Tiwar. *Religious Studies in the Pacific.* Colloquium Publications, 1978.

0839 Hinson, E. Glenn. "The Significance of Glossolalia in the History of Christianity," in *Speaking in Tongues: Let's Talk About It,* Watson E. Mills, editor. Word Books, 1973. Pp. 61–80.

0840 ______. "The Theory of Spirituality (Catholic-Baptist Comparison)," *OC* 17:3 (1981): 244–49.

0841 Hinton, John Howard. *The Work of the Holy Spirit in Conversion.* William Sands, 1834.

0842 Hirsch, Selma. *Die Vorstellung von einem weiblichen "pneuma hagion" im Neuen Testament und in der ältesten christlichen Literatur.* E. Eberling, 1926.

0843 Hobart, Alva Sabin. *Gifts, Fruits, and Fullness of the Spirit.* Christian Culture Press, 1898.

0844 ______. *The Holy Spirit: Our Silent Partner.* Revell Co., 1908.

0845 Hobbs, Herschel H. *The Holy Spirit: Believer's Guide.* Broadman Press, 1967.

0846 ______. "Tongues—Sign to Whom?" *HL* 19 (1976): 1.

0847 Hocken, Peter. "Jesus Christ and the Gifts of the Spirit," *P* 5:1 (Spring 1983): 1–16.

0848 Hodge, Caspar W. *The Witness of the Holy Spirit to the Bible.* Princeton University Press, 1913.

0849 Hodges, Melvin L. *Spiritual Gifts.* Gospel Publishing House, 1964.

0850 Hoedl, L. "Ich glaube an den Heiligen Geist, die Heilige Katholische Kirche: Zum Oekumenischen Verständnis des 3ten Glaubensartikels," *Cat* 36:3 (1982): 195–214.

0851 Hoekema, Anthony A. *Holy Spirit Baptism.* Eerdmans Publishing Co., 1972.

0852 ______. "Holy Spirit in Christian Experience," *RefR* 28 (Spring 1975): 183–91.

0853 ______. *Tongues and Spirit Baptism.* Baker Book House, 1970.

0854 ______. *What About Tongue-Speaking?* Eerdmans Publishing Co., 1966.

0855 Hoenderdaal, Gerrit Jan. *Geloven in de heilige Geest.* H. Veenman, 1968.

0856 Hoff, John L. "A Phenomenological Interpretation of the Doctrine of the Holy Spirit." Unpublished dissertation, Pacific School of Religion, 1966.

0857 Hoffman, James W. "Speaking in Tongues, 1963," *PL* 16 (September 1963): 14–17.

0858 Hoffman, Thomas A. "Inspiration, Normativeness, Canonicity, and the Unique Sacred Character of the Bible," *CBQ* 44 (July 1982): 447–69.

0859 Holdcroft, L. Thomas. *The Holy Spirit: A Pentecostal Interpretation.* Gospel Publishing House, 1979.

0860 Holden, George F. *The Holy Ghost: The Comforter.* Longmans, Green & Co., 1908.

0861 Hollenweger, Walter J. "Charismatic and Pentecostal Movements: a Challenge to the Churches," in *The Holy Spirit,* Dow Kirkpatrick, editor. Tidings, 1974. Pp. 209–33.

0862 ______. " 'Touching' and 'Thinking' the Spirit: Some Aspects of European Charismatics," in *Perspectives on the New Pentecostalism,* Russell P. Spittler, editor. Baker Book House, 1976. Pp. 44–50.

0863 Hollis, Arthur M. *The Fellowship of the Spirit.* Christian Literature Society for India, 1952.

0864 Holm, Bernard. "The Work of the Spirit: The Reformation to the Present," in *The Holy Spirit in the Life of the Church: From Biblical Times to the Present,* Paul D. Opsahl, editor. Augsburg Publishing Co., 1978. Pp. 99–136.

0865 Holotik, Gerhard. *Die pneumatische Note der Moraltheologie.* VWGÖ, 1984.

0866 Holwerda, David E. *The Holy Spirit and Eschatology in the Gospel of John.* J. H. Kok, 1959.

0867 "The Holy Ghost," *T* 76 (September 12, 1960): 71.

0868 Holy Ghost Fathers. *Devotion to God: The Holy Ghost.* Paraclete Press, 1954.

0869 "Holy Spirit and Charismatic Theology: Papers Given at a Conference Held at Western Theological Seminary, November 1974," *RefR* 28 (Spring 1975): 147–227.

0870 Hopko, Thomas. "On the Male Character of Christian Priesthood," *SVTQ* 19:3 (1975): 147–73.

0871 Hopwood, P. G. S. *The Religious Experience of the Primitive Church.* Scribner's, 1937.

0872 Horner, Jerry. "The Holy Spirit and the Wisdom of God," in *Essays on Apostolic Themes: Studies in Honor of Howard M. Ervin.* Paul Elbert, editor. Hendrickson Publishers, 1985. Pp. 82–91.

0873 Horner, Kenneth A. "A Study of the Spiritual Gifts with Special Attention to the Gift of Tongues." Unpublished thesis, Faith Theological Seminary, 1945.

0874 Hornig, Gottfried. "Der Perfektibilitätsgedanke bei J. S. Semler," *ZTK* 72:4 (1975): 381–97.

0875 Horton, Harold. *The Gifts of the Spirit.* Redemption Tidings Bookroom, 1946.

0876 Horton, Stanley M. "Old Testament Foundations of the Pentecostal Faith," *P* 1:1 (Spring 1979): 21–30.

0877 ______. *What the Bible Says About the Holy Spirit.* Gospel Publishing House, 1976.

0878 Hotrum, Ronald A. "An Inductive Study of the Old Testament on the Divine Spirit." Unpublished dissertation, Western Evangelical Seminary, 1971.

0879 Houghton, Thomas. *The Holy Spirit: His Deity, Personality, and Operations.* B. S. Taylor, 1937.

0880 Howard, David M. *By the Power of the Holy Spirit.* InterVarsity Press, 1973.

0881 Howe, John. *The Office and Work of the Holy Spirit.* Privately published, n.d.

0882 Howe, Leroy T. "Holy Spirit and Holy Church," *SLJ* 22 (December 1978): 43–57.

0883 ______. "Pentecostalism Today: Theological Reflections," *SEAJT* 18:1 (1977): 32–37.

0884 Hower, Robert George. "William Farel, Theologian of the Common Man, and the Genesis of Protestant Prayer (France, Switzerland)." Unpublished dissertation, Westminster Theological Seminary, 1983.

0885 Hoy, Albert L. "The Gift of Interpretation," *Para* 3 (Summer 1969): 28–31.

0886 Hoyle, Richard Birch. *The Holy Spirit in St. Paul.* Doubleday, Doran & Company, 1929.

0887 ______. "Paul's Doctrine of the Spirit," *BR* 13 (1928): 45–62.

0888 Hryniewicz, Waclaw. "Der pneumatologische Aspekt der Kirche aus Orthodoxer Sicht," *Cat* 31:2 (1977): 122–50.

0889 Hubbard, David A. *The Holy Spirit in Today's World.* Word Books, 1973.

0890 Huber, Christian Josef. *Seele des Leibes Christi: der Heilige Geist alleinender Lebensurgrund der Katholischen Kirche.* Edel, 1963.

0891 Huenemann, Edward M. "Of Divine Promise and the Holy Spirit: Theology Today and Tomorrow," *ChSoc* 70 (January-February 1980): 11–13.

0892 Huettenbuegel, Johannes. "Über Oekumenische Spiritualität," *Cat* 35:3 (1981): 211–22.

0893 Huffman, Jasper Abraham. *The Holy Spirit.* The Standard Press, 1944.

0894 ______. *The Meaning of Pentecost and the Spirit Filled Life.* The Standard Press, n.d.

0895 Hull, J. H. E. *The Holy Spirit in the Acts of the Apostles.* World Publishing Company, 1968.

0896 Hulme, William E. "New Life Through Caring Relationships in the Church," *WW* 2 (Fall 1982): 340–52.

0897 Humphreys, Fisher H. "Current Theological Trends Among Southern Baptists," *BHH* 15:3 (July 1980): 43–48.

0898 Hunt, Dwight. "Jesus' Teaching Concerning the Paraclete in the Upper Room Discourse." Unpublished dissertation, Western Conservative Baptist Seminary, 1981.

0899 Hunt, Earl G. *Storms and Starlight: Bishops' Messages on the Holy Spirit.* Tidings, 1974.

0900 Hunter, Harold D. *Spirit-Baptism: A Pentecostal Alternative.* University Press of America, 1983.

0901 Hurst, D. V. "How to Receive the Baptism with the Holy Ghost," *PE* (April 26, 1964): 7–9.

0902 Hutchings, William H. *The Person and Work of the Holy Ghost.* Longmans, Green & Co., 1897.

0903 Huxtable, William J. *The Promise of the Father.* Independent Press, 1959.

0904 Hynson, Leon O. "Church and Social Transformation: An Ethics of the Spirit," *WTJ* 11 (Spring 1976): 49–61.

I

0905 Idowu, E. Bolaji. "The Spirit of God in the Natural World," *WTJ* 17 (Fall 1982): 26–42.

0906 ______. "The Spirit of God in the Natural World," in *The Holy Spirit,* Dow Kirkpatrick, editor. Tidings, 1974. Pp. 9–19.

0907 Imakyure, Carl. "The Systems Approach and Local Church Renewal." Unpublished dissertation, Columbia University Teachers College, 1982.

0908 Inch, Morris A. *Saga of the Spirit: A Biblical, Systematic, and Historical Theology of the Holy Spirit.* Baker Book House, n.d.

0909 Ironside, Henry Allan. *The Mission of the Holy Spirit.* Loizeaux Brothers, 1928.

0910 ______. *Praying in the Holy Spirit.* Loizeaux Brothers, n.d.

0911 Irving, Edward. "On the Gift of the Holy Ghost," in *The Collected Writings of Edward Irving,* G. Carlyle, editor. 5 vols. A. Strahan, 1864. 5:509–61.

0912 Isaacs, M. E. *The Concept of Spirit: A Study of Pneuma in Hellenistic Judaism and Its Bearing on the New Testament.* Heythrop College, 1976.

0913 Ishii, Shigeo. "Led by the Power of the Spirit," *JCQ* 42 (Fall 1976): 200.

0914 Israel, Martin. *Smouldering Fire: The Work of the Holy Spirit.* Crossroad, 1981.

0915 It, Chin Ban. "The Spiritual Gifts," in *Bishop's Move,* Michael Harper, editor. Hodder & Stoughton, 1978. Pp. 137–60.

0916 Ittel, Gerhard Wolfgang. "Die Hauptgedanken der 'Religionsgeschichtlichen Schule,'" *ZRGG* 10 (1958): 61–78.

0917 Itterzon, G. P. van. "Het filioque in de latere kerkgeschiedenis," in *De Spiritu Sancto.* Kemick, 1964. Pp. 89–108.

0918 Ivens, T. L. *The Essence of Confirmation—the Gift.* Privately published, n.d.

0919 Ivey, Olin M. "The Concept of the Holy Spirit in the Thought of Carl Michaelson." Unpublished dissertation, Claremont Graduate School, 1974.

0920 ______. "Toward a Contemporary Understanding of the Holy Spirit," *DG* 45:1 (1974–1975): 131–57.

J

0921 Jackson, Charles B. "The Progressive Revelation of the Idea of the Spirit of God in the Old Testament." Unpublished dissertation, Southern Baptist Seminary, 1925.

0922 Jackson, F. J. and Kirsopp Lake, eds. "The Development of Thought on the Spirit, the Church, and Baptism," *BC* 1 (1920): 321–44.

0923 Jackson, George Denning. "The Biblical Basis of the Theology of P. T. Forsyth." Unpublished dissertation, Princeton Theological Seminary, 1952.

0924 Jackson, Thomas, ed. *The Works of John Wesley.* 14 vols. Zondervan, 1959.

0925 Jacob, Punnackal J. "The Motherhood of the Holy Spirit," *JD* 5 (April-June 1980): 160–74.

0926 Jaeger, Werner W. *Gregor von Nyssa's Lehre vom Heiligen Geist.* E. J. Brill, 1966.

0927 James, Maynard G. *I Believe in the Holy Ghost.* Bethany Press, 1965.

0928 Janson, W. J. M. "The Guidance of the Spirit," in *The Spirit in Biblical Perspective,* W. S. Vorster, editor. University of South Africa, 1980. Pp. 82–95.

0929 Janssen, William Peter. "The Implications of the Doctrine of the Holy Spirit for Counseling." Unpublished dissertation, Fuller Theological Seminary, 1973.

0930 Jarrett, Bede. *The Abiding Presence of the Holy Ghost in the Soul.* Westminster Press, 1943.

0931 Jeffords, Raymond. "The Human Soul. A Baha'i Perspective," *WO* 17:1 (Fall 1982): 37–44.

0932 Jeffries, John Campbell. *This Same Jesus: Doctrine of the Holy Spirit.* Exposition Press, 1950.

0933 Jenkyn, Thomas William. *The Union of the Holy Spirit and the Church in the Conversion of the World.* Gould, Kendall, and Lincoln, 1846.

0934 Jensen, Jerry, ed. *Baptists and the Baptism of the Holy Spirit.* Full Gospel Business Men's Fellowship International, 1963.

0935 ______. *Catholics and the Baptism in the Holy Spirit.* Full Gospel Business Men's Fellowship International, 1968.

0936 ______. *Charisma in the 20th Century Church.* Full Gospel Business Men's Fellowship International, 1968.

0937 ______. *The Lutherans and the Baptism of the Holy Spirit.* Full Gospel Business Men's Fellowship International, 1963.

0938 ______. *Methodists and the Baptism of the Holy Spirit.* Full Gospel Business Men's Fellowship International, 1963.

0939 ______. *Physicians Examine the Baptism in the Holy Spirit.* Full Gospel Business Men's Fellowship International, 1967.

0940 ______. *Presbyterians and the Baptism of the Holy Spirit.* Full Gospel Business Men's Fellowship International, 1963.

0941 Jepson, Julius Walter. *What You Should Know about the Holy Spirit.* Bible Voice Books, 1975.

0942 Jervell, Jacob. "Den Oppstandnes and Talen om den Hellige and I Det Nye Testamente," *NTTid* 77:1 (1976): 19–32.

0943 Jetter, Werner. *Über den Geist.* Mohr, 1968.

0944 Johansson, Nils. *Parakletoi: Vorstellungen von Fürspecher für die Menschen vor Gott in der alttestamentlichen Religion, im Spätjudentum und Urchristentum.* Gleerup, 1940.

0945 John, of Saint Thomas, with Dominic Hughes (trans.). *The Gifts of the Holy Ghost.* Sheed & Ward, 1951.

0946 Johnson, Ashley Sidney. *The Holy Spirit and the Human Mind.* Gaut-Ogden Company, 1903.

0947 Johnson, Cedric B. "Process of Change: Sacred and Secular," *JPTh* 5 (Spring 1977): 103–9.

0948 Johnson, Elias Henry. *The Holy Spirit Then and Now.* The Griffith and Rowland Press, 1904.

0949 Johnson, Maxwell E. "The Paschal Mystery: Reflections from a Lutheran Viewpoint," *Wor* 57 (March 1983): 134–50.

0950 Johnston, George. " 'Spirit' and 'Holy Spirit' in the Qumran Literature," in *New Testament Sidelights: Essays in Honor of Alexander Con-*

verse Purdy, Harvey K. McArthur, editor. Hartford Seminary Press, 1960. Pp. 27–42.

0951 ______. *The Spirit-Paraclete in the Gospel of John.* Cambridge University Press, 1970.

0952 Jones, A. B. "Consciousness and Its Relation to the Holy Spirit," in *A Symposium on the Holy Spirit.* John Burns, 1879. Pp. 1–36.

0953 Jones, A. B., T. Munnell, G. W. Longan, J. Taylor, and A. Campbell. *A Symposium of the Holy Spirit.* John Burns, 1879.

0954 Jones, J. Ithel. "Holy Spirit," *ExT* 69 (May 1958): 246.

0955 ______. *The Holy Spirit and Christian Preaching.* Epworth, 1967.

0956 ______. "The Holy Spirit in Christian Proclamation." Unpublished dissertation, Southern Baptist Seminary, 1965.

0957 ______. "Intoxication (Sermon, Whitsunday; Acts 2:15)," *ExT* 66 (May 1955): 245–46.

0958 Jones, James W. *The Spirit and the World.* Hawthorn Books, 1975.

0959 Jorstad, Erling, T., ed. *The Holy Spirit in Today's Church: A Handbook on the New Pentecostalism.* Abingdon Press, 1973.

0960 Jossua, Jean-Pierre. "Theologie—enen gave van de Geest?" in *Leven uit de geest.* Hilversum, 1974. Pp. 211–23.

0961 ______. "Theology, Charism of the Spirit?" in *Experience of the Spirit,* edited by Peter Huizing and William Bassett. Seabury Press, 1974. Pp. 10–19.

0962 Joy, Donald M. "The Biblical Idea of the Confirming Presence," in *The Word and the Doctrine,* Kenneth E. Geiger, editor. Beacon Hill Press, 1965. Pp. 247–56.

0963 ______. *The Holy Spirit and You.* Light and Life Press, 1965.

0964 Juhasz, Istvan. "Dumitru Staniloae's Ecumenical Studies as an Aspect of the Orthodox-Protestant Dialogue," *JES* 16 (Fall 1979): 747–64.

0965 Jungkuntz, Theodore. "Sectarian Consequences of Mistranslation in Luther's Smalcald Articles," *CTM* 4 (1977): 166–67.

0966 Jyrwa, J. Fortis. "Christianity in Khasi Culture: A Study of the Relationship Between Christianity and Traditional Khasi Culture with Special Reference to the Seng Khasi Movement from 1899 to 1983." Unpublished dissertation, Fuller Theological Seminary, School of World Mission, 1984.

K

0967 Käsemann, Ernst. "Der Gottesdienstliche Schrei Nach der Freiheit (Rom 8)," *ZNW* 3: (1964): 142–55.

0968 Kagawa, Toyohiko, with Charles A. Logan (trans.). *Meditations on the Holy Spirit.* Cokesbury, 1939.

0969 Kahnie, Karl F. *Die Lehre vom Heiligen Geist.* H. Schmidt, 1847.

0970 Kaiser, Christopher B. "Discernment of Triunity," *SJT* 28:5 (1975): 449–60.

0971 Kaitschuk, John Paul. "The Pastor as an Enabler: A Study of the Relationship Between the Pastor and the Congregation of Trinity Lutheran Church, Olney, Illinois." Unpublished dissertation, Drew University, 1980.

0972 Kandler, Karl H. "Abendmahl und Heiliger Geist (zu Neueren Bilateralen Lehrgesprächen)," *KD* 28 (July-September 1982): 215–28.

0973 Kann, Herbert E. "The Holy Spirit and His Relation to Christ as Found in the Four Gospels." Unpublished dissertation, Dallas Seminary, 1952.

0974 Kapelrud, Arvid S. "Anden og Ordet I Profetenes Forkynnelse," *NTTid* 77:1 (1978): 1–17.

0975 Karpp, Heinrich. *Schrift und Geist bei Tertullian.* C. Bertelsmann, 1955.

0976 Kasper, Walter. "Aspekte gegenwärtiger Pneumatologie," in *Gegenwart des Geistes: Aspekte der Pneumatologie,* Walter Kasper, editor. Herder, 1979. Pp. 7–22.

0977 ______. "Geest—Christus—Kerk," in *Leven uit de geest.* Hilversum, 1974. Pp. 46–64.

0978 ______. *Gegenwart des Geistes: Aspekte der Pneumatologie.* Herder, 1979.

0979 ______. "Ministry in the Church: Taking Issue with Edward Schillebeeckx," *Com* 10 (Summer 1983): 185–95.

0980 Keefer, Luke L., Jr. "John Wesley: Disciple of Early Christianity." Unpublished dissertation, Temple University, 1982.

0981 Keen, S. A. *Pentecostal Papers or the Gift of the Holy Ghost.* M. W. Knapp, 1896.

0982 ______. *Pentecostal Sanctification.* West Publishing Company, n.d.

0983 Kehl, Medard. "Kirche—Sakrament des Geistes," in *Gegenwart des Geistes: Aspekte der Pneumatologie,* Walter Kasper, editor. Herder, 1979. Pp. 155–80.

0984 Keiper, R. L. *Tongues and the Holy Spirit.* Moody Press, 1963.

0985 Keithly, J. W. *The Mission of the Holy Spirit.* Jennings, 1903.

0986 Kellett, Norman Lawrence. "John Wesley and the Restoration of the Doctrine of the Holy Spirit to the Church of England in the Eighteenth-Century." Unpublished dissertation, Brandeis University, 1975.

0987 Kelly, Bernard J. *The Seven Gifts.* Sheed & Ward, 1941.

0988 Kelly, William. *Lectures on the New Testament Doctrine of the Holy Spirit.* W. H. Broom, 1868.

0989 Kendall, E. Lorna. "Speaking with Tongues," *CQR* 168 (January-March 1967): 11–19.

0990 Kennedy, William Bean. "The Genesis and Development of the Christian Faith and Life Series." Unpublished dissertation, Yale University, 1957.

0991 Kenyon, John B. *The Bible Revelation of the Holy Spirit.* Zondervan, 1939.

0992 Kephart, Isaiah L. *The Holy Spirit in the Devout Life.* United Brethren Publishing House, 1904.

0993 Kern, Walter. "Philosophische Pneumatologie. Zur theologischen Aktualität Hegels," in *Gegenwart des Geistes: Aspekte der Pneumatologie,* Walter Kasper, editor. Herder, 1979. P. 54.

0994 Kesich, Veselin. "Resurrection, Ascension, and the Giving of the Spirit," *GOTR* 25 (Fall 1980): 249–60.

0995 Ketcherside, W. Carl. *Heaven Help Us: The Holy Spirit in Your Life.* New Life Books, 1974.

0996 Khodre, Georges. "The Economy of the Holy Spirit," in *Faith Meets Faith,* Gerald H. Anderson, editor. Paulist Press, 1981. Pp. 36–49.

0997 Kildahl, J. A. *Misconceptions of the Word and Work of the Holy Spirit.* Augsburg Publishing Co., 1927.

0998 Kildahl, John N. *The Holy Spirit and Our Faith.* Augsburg Publishing Co., 1960.

0999 Kilmartin, Edward J. "The Active Role of Christ and the Holy Spirit in the Sanctification of the Eucharistic Elements," *ThSt* 45 (June 1984): 225–53.

1000 ______. "The Active role of Christ and the Spirit in the Divine Liturgy," *Diak* 17:2 (1982): 95–108.

1001 Kim, Borok P. "The Role of the Holy Spirit in the Modality of Christ's Presence in the Eucharist in the Thought of Francois-Xavier Durrwell." Unpublished dissertation, Fordham University, 1978.

1002 Kim, Paul Shu. "A Study of Ministry to Second Generation Korean Immigrants in the Church." Unpublished dissertation, Drew University, 1980.

1003 Kim, Seung Lak. "John Wesley's Doctrine of the Witness of the Spirit, or, the Assurance of Salvation." Unpublished dissertation, Southern Baptist Seminary, 1932.

1004 Kim, Young O. *Unification Theology.* Holy Spirit Association for the Unification of World Christianity, 1980.

1005 Kinder, Ernst. "Zur Lehre vom Heiligen Geist nach den Lutherischen Bekenntnisschriften," *Ful* 15 (1964): 7–38.

1006 King, Rachel Hadley. *The Omission of the Holy Spirit from Reinhold Niebuhr's Theology.* Philosophical Library, 1964.

1007 Kinghorn, Kenneth C. *Fresh Wind of the Spirit.* Abingdon Press, 1975.

1008 Kinlaw, Dennis F., William C. Cessna, and Gilbert M. James. *The Sanctified Life.* Asbury Theological Seminary, 1968.

1009 Kipp, John Lewis. "The Relationship Between the Conceptions of 'Holy Spirit' and 'Risen Christ' in the Fourth Gospel: A Study of John 1–20." Unpublished dissertation, Princeton Theological Seminary, 1967.

1010 Kirk, Martin Joseph. "The Spirituality of Isaac Thomas Hecker Reconciling the American Character and the Catholic Faith." Unpublished dissertation, St. Louis University, 1980.

1011 Kirkpatrick, Dow. *The Holy Spirit (5th Oxford Institute on Methodist Theological Studies, 1973)*. Tidings, 1974.

1012 Kjeseth, Peter Lars. *The Final Act: The Role of the Holy Spirit in the Life of God's People*. Augsburg Publishing Co., 1967.

1013 ______. "The Spirit of Power: A Study of the Holy Spirit in Luke–Acts." Unpublished dissertation, University of Chicago, 1967.

1014 Klein, Jean Louis. "Esprit et l'Ecriture," *ETR* 51:2 (1976): 149–63.

1015 Kluepfer, P. *The Holy Spirit in the Life and Teachings of Jesus and the Early Christian Church*. Lutheran Book Concern, 1929.

1016 Knight, G. A. F. *A Biblical Approach to the Doctrine of the Trinity*. Oliver and Boyd, 1953.

1017 Knight, John A. "John Fletcher's Influence on the Development of Wesleyan Theology in America," *WTJ* 13 (Spring 1978): 13–33.

1018 Knoebel, Thomas Louis. "Grace in the Theology of Karl Rahner: A Systematic Presentation." Unpublished dissertation, Fordham University, 1980.

1019 Köberle, J. *Natur und Geist nach der Auffassung des alten Testaments*. Munich, 1901.

1020 Kocher, M. "Présupposés d'une pneumatologie charismatique Recherche en théologie réformée" (part 1), *Hok* 23 (1983): 49–60.

1021 ______. "Présupposés d'une pneumatologie charismatique Recherche en théologie réformée" (part 2), *Hok* 24 (1983): 9–32.

1022 Koch, Roy S. "Filled with the Spirit," in *Encounter with the Holy Spirit*, George R. Brunk, II, editor. Herald Press, 1972. Pp. 101–13.

1023 Koehn, Allen Dean. "Individual Responsibility in the Light of the Sovereignty of the Holy Spirit." Unpublished dissertation, Fuller Theological Seminary, 1975.

1024 Koenig, John. *Charismata: God's Gift for God's People*. Westminster Press, 1978.

1025 ______. "From Mystery to Ministry: Paul as Interpreter of Charismatic Gifts," *USQR* 33:3/4 (1978): 167–74.

1026 ______. "Minneapolis: 1974 Conference on the Holy Spirit," *LW* 21:4 (1974): 396–99.

1027 Koernke, Theresa F. "The Pneumatological Dimension of the Eucharist: The Contribution of Modern Catholic Theology to the

Relationship between Office, Eucharist and Holy Spirit." Unpublished dissertation, University of Notre Dame, 1983.

1028 Kolipinski, Stanislas J. *Le don de l'Esprit Saint.* Bureaus des Studia Friburgensia, 1924.

1029 Kölling, Wilhelm. *Pneumatologie: oder, Die Lehre von der Person des heiligen Geistes.* C. Bortelsmann, 1894.

1030 Krause, H.-J. *Heiliger Geist: Gottes befreiende Gegenwart.* Kösel, 1986.

1031 Kremer, Jacob. *Les Actes des Apôtres: Traditons, Rédaction, Théologie.* J. Duculot, 1979.

1032 ______. *Pfingstbericht und Pfingstgeschehen: Eine Exegetische Untersuchung zu Apg. 2,1-13.* KBW Verlag, 1974.

1033 ______. *Pfingsten: Erfahrung des Geistes.* KBW Verlag, 1974.

1034 Kremkau, Klaus, ed. *Das Religiöse Bewusstsein und der Heilige Geist in der Kirche.* Otto Lembeck, 1980.

1035 Krentz, Edgar. "The Spirit in Pauline and Johannine Theology," in *The Holy Spirit in the Life of the Church: From Biblical Times to the Present,* Paul D. Opsahl, editor. Augsburg Publishing Co., 1978. Pp. 47–65.

1036 Kretschmar, Georg. "Der Heilige Geist in der Geschichte. Grundzüge frühchristlicher Pneumatologie," in *Gegenwart des Geistes: Aspekte der Pneumatologie,* Walter Kasper, editor. Herder, 1979. Pp. 92–131.

1037 Krodel, Gerhard. "An Exegetical Examination," *Dia* 2 (1963): 154–56.

1038 ______. "The Functions of the Spirit in the Old Testament, the Synoptic Tradition, and the Book of Acts," in *The Holy Spirit in the Life of the Church: From Biblical Times to the Present,* Paul D. Opsahl, editor. Augsburg Publishing Co., 1978. Pp. 10–46.

1039 Krusche, W. *Das Wirken des Heiligen Geistes nach Calvin.* Vandenhoeck & Ruprecht, 1957.

1040 Kuderer, Peter. *Im Heiligen Geiste: Kleine Theologie des Geistes Gottes.* Herder, 1940.

1041 Kühn, Bernhard, ed. *Die Pfingstbewegung im Lichte der Heiligen Schrift und ihrer eigenen Geschichte.* Missionbuchhandlung P. Ott, n.d.

1042 ______. "Zur Unterscheidung der Geister," in *Die sog. Pfingstbewegung,* H. Dallmeyer, editor. N.p., 1922. Pp. 23–40.

1043 Kumar, B. J. Christie. "An Indian Christian Appreciation of the Doctrine of the Holy Spirit: A Search into the Religious Heritage of the Indian Christian," *IJT* 30 (January-March 1981): 29–35.

1044 Küng, Hans. "Confirmation as the Completion of Baptism," in *Experience of the Spirit,* Peter Huizing and William Bassett, editors. Seabury Press, 1974. Pp. 79–99.

1045 ______. "Het vormsel als voltooiing van de doop," in *Leven uit de geest.* Hilversum, 1974. Pp. 105–13.

1046 Küng, Hans and Jürgen Moltmann, eds. *Conflicts about the Holy Spirit.* Seabury Press, 1979.

1047 Kuyper, Abraham. *The Work of the Holy Spirit.* (Reprint) Eerdmans Publishing Co., 1964.

1048 Kwiran, Manfred. "Der Heilige Geist als Stiefkind: Bemerkungen zur Confessio Augustana," *ThZ* 31 (July-August 1975): 223–36.

1049 Kydd, Ronald A. N. *Charismatic Gifts in the Early Church.* Hendrickson Publishers, 1986.

L

1050 La Barge, Joseph Albert. "The Notion of the Assistance of the Holy Spirit in the Ecclesiology of Johann Baptist Franzelin." Unpublished dissertation, Catholic University of America, 1971.

1051 Laberge, Leo. "Ministères et Esprit dans les Communautes Post-exiliques," *EgTh* 9 (October 1978): 379–411.

1052 Lachat, William. *La réception et l'action du Saint-Esprit.* Delachaux & Niestlé, 1953.

1053 Lady, Jesse F. "The Holy Spirit in the New Testament," in *Insights into Holiness,* Kenneth Geiger, editor. Beacon Hill Press, 1966. Pp. 101–10.

1054 Laird, Robert M. *A Discourse on the Witnessing of the Holy Spirit.* J. S. Zieber, 1831.

1055 Lakin, B. R. *The Doctrine of the Holy Spirit: His Person and Work, His Threefold Mission.* Tabernacle, n.d.

1056 Lambert, Charles E. *Life in the Spirit.* SPCK, 1951.

1057 Lambert, J. C. "Spiritual Gifts," in *The International Standard Bible Encyclopedia.* 5 vols. Howard-Severance Company, 1915. 5:2843–44.

1058 Laminski, Adolf. *Der Heilige Geist als Geist Christi und Geist der Gläubigen.* St. Benno-Verlag, 1969.

1059 Lampe, G. W. H. "On Baptism and the Spirit," in *Saint Paul: Teacher and Traveller,* Ivor Bulmer-Thomas, editor. Faith Press, 1975. Pp. 107–14.

1060 ______. *God as Spirit.* Oxford University Press, 1977.

1061 ______. "The Holy Spirit in the Writings of Saint Luke," in *Studies in the Gospels: Essays in Memory of R. H. Lightfoot,* D. E. Nineham, editor. Oxford University Press, 1957. Pp. 159–201.

1062 ______. *The Seal of the Spirit.* Longmans, Green & Co., 1951.

1063 Landau, Rudolf. " 'Komm, Heiliger Geist, du Tröster Wert': Gestaltungen des Heiligen Geistes," *EvTh* 41 (May-June 1981): 187–211.

1064 Landis, Paul G. "The Holy Spirit and Prayer," in *Encounter with the Holy Spirit,* George R. Brunk, II, editor. Herald Press, 1972. Pp. 221–304.

1065 Langford, Thomas A. "The Holy Spirit and Sanctification: Refinding the Lost Image of Creation," in *The Holy Spirit,* Dow Kirkpatrick, editor. Tidings, 1974. Pp. 187–203.

1066 Lanne, Emmanuel. "Congres Théologique International de Pneumatologie (Mr 22–26 1982; Vatican; Rpt)," *Iren* 55:2 (1982): 235–40.

1067 Laporte, Jean. "The Holy Spirit, Source of Life and Activity in the Early Church," in *Perspectives on Charismatic Renewal,* Edward D. O'Connor, editor. University of Notre Dame Press, 1975. Pp. 57–99.

1068 "La Renovacion Carismatica de la Iglesia: Perspectivas del Nuevo Testamento," *EsTe* 3 (July-December 1976): 65–84.

1069 Lashure, Richard Lee. "Spirit of God: A Study of Karl Barth's Doctrine of the Holy Spirit and Its Application." Unpublished dissertation, School of Theology at Claremont, 1976.

1070 Laski, Margharita. *Ecstasy: A Study of Some Secular and Religious Experiences.* Indiana University Press, 1961.

1071 Latuihamallo, Peter D. "Response to the Willowbank Report on Gospel and Culture," *SEAJT* 19:2 (1978): 50–62.

1072 Law, William. *Power of the Spirit.* James Nisbet & Company, 1896.

1073 Lawrence, John Benjamin. *The Holy Spirit in Evangelism.* Zondervan, 1954.

1074 ______. *The Holy Spirit in Missions.* Home Mission Board of Southern Baptist Convention, 1947.

1075 ______. *Power for Service.* C. O. Chalmers, 1909.

1076 Lawrence, William Frank, Jr. "The History of the Interpretation of Acts 8:26–40 by the Church Fathers Prior to the Fall of

Rome." Unpublished dissertation, Union Theological Seminary, 1984.

1077 Lawson, Arvest Neal. "A Program for Renewal and Outreach in Amboy United Methodist Church in Light of John Wesley's Thought." Unpublished dissertation, Drew University, 1983.

1078 Lazarotto, Angelo S. *The Catholic Church in China*. Holy Spirit Study Centre, 1982.

1079 Leavell, Landrum P. *The Doctrine of the Holy Spirit*. Convention Press, 1983.

1080 LeBarron, Albert. "A Case of Psychic Automation, Including 'Speaking with Tongues' " *Proceedings of the Society for Psychical Research* 12 (1896–1897): 277.

1081 Lechler, Karl von. *Die biblische Lehre vom Heiligen Geiste*. C. Bertelsmann, 1899.

1082 Lederle, H. I. "Be Filled with the Spirit of Love: An Update on the State of the Charismatic Renewal and Some Reflections on its Central Experiential Teaching," *ThEv* 15:3 (December 1982): 33–48.

1083 ______. *Treasures Old and New. Interpretations of Spirit-Baptism in the Charismatic Renewal Movement*. Hendrickson, 1988.

1084 Leen, Edward. *The Holy Ghost and His Work in Souls*. Sheed & Ward, 1938.

1085 Lefebvre, Gaspar. *The Spirit of God in the Liturgy*. Burns, Oates & Washbourne, 1959.

1086 ______. *The Spirit of Worship*. Hawthorn Books, 1959.

1087 Le Guillon, Marie J. *Les témoins sont parmi nous: l'experience de Dieu dans l'Esprit-Saint*. Fayard, 1976.

1088 Lehman, Chester K. *The Holy Spirit and the Holy Life*. Herald Press, 1959.

1089 Lehmann, Karl. "Heiliger Geist, Befreiung zum Menschsein—Teilhabe am göttlichen Leben. Tendenzen gegenwärtiger Gnadenlehre," in *Gegenwart des Geistes: Aspekte der Pneumatologie,* Walter Kasper, editor. Herder, 1979. Pp. 181–204.

1090 Leimgruber, Stephan. *Das Sprechen vom Geist*. Benziger, 1978.

1091 Leisegang, Hans. *Pneuma Hagion*. J. C. Hinrichs, 1972.

1092 Leisering, Katherine Jane. "An Historical and Critical Study of the Pittsburgh Preaching Career of Kathryn Kuhlman." Unpublished dissertation, Ohio University, 1981.

1093 Lengeling, E. J. "Per istam sanctam unctionem—adiuvet te Dominus gratia Spiritus Sancti" in *Lex Orandi, Lex Credendi,* Gerardo J. Békés and Giustino Farnedi, editors. Editrice Anselmiana, 1980. Pp. 79–80.

1094 Lensink, Johan Marie. "The Gospel in the Context of Black Migratory Labour: An Inquiry into the Present Relevance of the Gospel Message and Possible New Ways of Preaching." Unpublished dissertation, University of South Africa, 1979.

1095 Lescrauwaet, Jos. "Ter inleiding: Theoloog van een geloofsgemeenschap," in *Leven uit de geest.* Hilversum, 1974. Pp. 10–16.

1096 Lesser, R. H. *The Holy Spirit and the Charismatic Renewal.* Theological Publications in India, 1978.

1097 Leuba, Jean Louis. "Der Zusammenhang zwischen Geist und Tradition nach dem Neuen Testament," *KD* 4 (1958): 234–50.

1098 Lewis, Arthur H. "The New Birth Under the Old Covenant." *EQ* 56 (January 1984): 35–44.

1099 Lewis, Edwin. *The Ministry of the Holy Spirit.* Tidings, 1954.

1100 Lewis, Enoch. *Essay on Baptism: Showing that the Baptism of the Spirit and Not with Water is the True Christian Baptism.* U. Hunt, 1839.

1101 Lewis, I. M. *Ecstatic Religion: An Anthropological Study of Spirit Possession and Shamanism.* Pelican Books, 1971.

1102 Lewis, John. "The Spirit in the Religious Life," in *Bishop's Move,* Michael Harper, editor. Hodder & Stoughton, 1978. Pp. 101–20.

1103 Lewis, Walter England. "Help One Another Make Him Known—Equipping the Laity to Share the Good News." Unpublished dissertation, Drew University, 1983.

1104 Lewis, Warren. *Witness to the Holy Spirit: An Anthology.* Judson Press, 1978.

1105 Limbeck, M. "Pfingsten: Der Hl. Geist und die Kirche," *LS* 10 (1969): 232–45.

1106 Lindars, Barnabas and Stephen S. Smalley. *Christ and Spirit in the New Testament: In Honour of Charles Francis Digby Moule.* Cambridge University Press, 1973.

1107 Lindberg, Carter. *The Third Reformation? Charismatic Movements and the Lutheran Tradition.* Mercer University Press, 1983.

1108 Linde, Simon van der. "De betekenis van de Heilige Geest in het spiritualistisch Piëtisme van de Labadisten," in *De Spiritu Sancto.* Kemick, 1964. Pp. 151–79.

1109 ______. *De leer van den Heiligen Geist bij Calvijn.* H. Veenman, 1943.

1110 Lindsay, Gordon. *All About the Gifts of the Spirit.* N.p., n.d.

1111 Lindsell, Harold. *The Holy Spirit in the Latter Days.* Nelson, 1983.

1112 ______. "Spiritual Gifts: A Biblical Perspective on What They Are and Who Has Them (1 Cor 12:4–11)," *CT* 19 (April 11, 1975): 5–7.

1113 Locher, Gottfried W. "Der Geist als Paraklet: Eine exegetischdogmatische Besinnung," *EvTh* 26 (1966): 565–79.

1114 ______. *Testimonium internum: Calvins Lehre vom Heiligen Geist und das hermeneutische Problem.* Evangelisches Verlag, 1964.

1115 Lockyer, Herbert. *The Gift of Pentecost: The Person and Power of the Holy Spirit.* Parry Jackman, 1956.

1116 ______. *The Holy Spirit of God.* Nelson, 1981.

1117 Loen, A. E. "De Heilige Geest volgens het idealisme," in *De Spiritu Sancto.* Kemick, 1964. Pp. 180–206.

1118 Loewen, Jacob A. "Clean Air or Bad Breath (Translating Concept of Spirit in African Languages)," *BibTr* 34:2 (April 1983): 213–19.

1119 Lofthouse, William F. *The Father and the Son: A Study in Johannine Thought.* N.p., 1934.

1120 ______. "The Holy Spirit in the Acts and the Fourth Gospel," *ExT* 52 (1940–1941): 334–36.

1121 Lonergan, Bernard. "Evangelisch reveil en aanwezigheid van de Geest in de 12e en 13e eeuw," in *Leven uit de geest.* Hilversum, 1974. Pp. 145–49.

1122 ______. "Mission and the Spirit," in *Experience of the Spirit,* Peter Huizing and William Bassett, editors. Seabury Press, 1974. Pp. 69–78.

1123 ______. "Zending en de Geest," in *Leven uit de geest.* Hilversum, 1974. Pp. 132–44.

1124 Longan, G. W. "The Holy Spirit in Consciousness," in *A Symposium on the Holy Spirit.* John Burns, 1879. Pp. 37–78.

1125 Lonning, Inge. "Laeren om den Hellige," *NTTid* 77:4 (1976): 227–43.

1126 López, Rafael. *El Espíritu Santo: Supremo consolador del sacerdote.* Editorial La Cruz, 1979.

1127 Lovett, Miller Currier. "The Doctrine of the Holy Spirit in Adult Church School Literature of the Methodist Church: 1941–1963." Unpublished dissertation, Boston University Graduate School, 1964.

1128 Lowry, Oscar. *The Pentecostal Baptism and the Enduement of Power.* Moody Press, 1936.

1129 Loyd, Philip H. *The Holy Spirit in the Acts.* Mowbrays, 1952.

1130 Luislampe, Pia. *Spiritus vivificans: Grundzüge einer Theologie des Heiligen Geistes nach Basilius von Caesarea.* Aschendorff, 1981.

1131 Lull, David John. " 'Pneuma' in Paul's Letter to the Churches of Galatia: An Interpretation of the Spirit in Light of Early Christian Experience in Galatia." Unpublished dissertation, Claremont, 1978.

1132 ______. "The Spirit and the Creative Transformation of Human Existence," *JAAR* 47 (March 1979): 39–55.

1133 Lumsden, Clarence B. "The Spirit in Paul and John." Unpublished dissertation, Yale University, 1932.

1134 Lundgren, Ivar. "Lewi Pethrus and the Swedish Pentecostal Movement," in *Essays on Apostolic Themes: Studies in Honor of Howard M. Ervin.* Paul Elbert, editor. Hendrickson Publishers, 1985. Pp. 158–72.

1135 Lütgert, Wilhelm. *Gottes Sohn und Gottes Geist: Vorträge zur Christologie und zur Lehre vom Geiste Gottes.* Deichert, 1905.

1136 *Lutherans, the Spirit, the Gifts, and the World.* Privately published, 1973.

1137 Lyon, Robert W. "Baptism and Spirit Baptism in the New Testament," *WTJ* 14 (Spring 1979): 14–26.

1138 Lyons, Adrian. *Come, O Holy Ghost!* Clonmore & Reynolds, 1957.

M

1139 Macaskill, Peter Macintosh. "The Spirit's Work in the Believer's Life According to the Pauline Letters." Unpublished master's thesis, Princeton University, 1948.

1140 Macaulay, Joseph Cordner. *Life in the Spirit as Exemplified in the Acts of the Apostles.* Eerdmans Publishing Co., 1955.

1141 McCallum, Floyd F. "Psychological Orientation in Spiritual Discernment," in *Further Insights into Holiness,* Kenneth Geiger, editor. Beacon Hill Press, 1963. Pp. 315–32.

1142 McCann, Forrest Mason. "The Development of the Hymn in Old and Middle English Literature." Unpublished dissertation, Texas Tech University, 1980.

1143 McCarthy, David S. *Our Constant Companion: God in Three Persons Watches Over Us.* Judson Press, 1984.

1144 McCasland, S. V. "Spirit," in *Interpreter's Dictionary of the Bible,* George Arthur Buttrick, editor. Abingdon Press, 1962. R-Z: 432–33.

1145 McClenny, L. Poindexter. "Life in the Spirit." Unpublished dissertation, Dallas Theological Seminary, 1952.

1146 McClimans, John. "A Comparison of the Wesleyan and Keswickian Interpretations of the Work of the Holy Spirit in Believers." Unpublished dissertation, Western Evangelical Seminary, 1957.

1147 McClure, A. D. *Another Comforter: A Study of the Mission of the Holy Spirit.* Revell Co., 1897.

1148 McCone, R. Clyde. *Culture and Controversy: An Investigation of the Tongues of Pentecost.* Dorrance, 1978.

1149 McConkey, James H. *The Three-Fold Secret of the Holy Spirit*. F. Kelker, 1897.

1150 McConkie, Oscar W. *The Holy Ghost*. Deseret Book Company, 1944.

1151 McConnell, F. J. *John Wesley*. Abingdon-Cokesbury, 1939.

1152 McCown, Wayne. "God's Will for You: Sanctification in the Thessalonian Epistles," *WTJ* 12 (Spring 1977): 26–33.

1153 McCrossan, Thomas J. *Are All Christians Baptized with the Holy Ghost at Conversion?* Privately published, 1932.

1154 ______. *Speaking with Other Tongues: Sign or Gift—Which?* Christian Alliance Publishing Co., 1919.

1155 McCulloch, Roy R. "The Holy Spirit: The Interpreter of Jesus." Unpublished dissertation, Southern Baptist Seminary, 1927.

1156 MacDonald, Allan J. M. *The Interpreter Spirit and Human Life: A Study of the Doctrine of the Holy Spirit in the Old Testament, the Wisdom Books, and the New Testament*. SPCK, 1944.

1157 MacDonald, William G. *Another Comforter: The Person and Mission of the Holy Spirit*. McDonald, Gill & Company, 1890.

1158 MacDonald, William Graham. "Problems of Pneumatology in Christology: The Relationship of Christ and the Holy Spirit in Biblical Theology." Unpublished dissertation, Southern Baptist Seminary, 1970.

1159 ______. "The Significance of Glossolalia in Neo-Pentecostalism," in *Speaking in Tongues: Let's Talk About It*, Watson E. Mills, editor. Word Books, 1973. Pp. 81–93.

1160 McDonnell, Kilian. *Baptism in the Spirit as an Ecumenical Problem*. University of Notre Dame Press, 1972.

1161 ______. "The Determinative Doctrine of the Holy Spirit," *ThTo* 39 (July 1982): 142–61.

1162 ______. "The Distinguishing Characteristics of the Charismatic-Pentecostal Spirituality," *OC* 10:2 (1974): 117–28.

1163 ______. "The Experience of the Holy Spirit in the Catholic Charismatic Renewal," in *Conflicts about the Holy Spirit*, Hans Küng and Jürgen Moltmann, editors. Seabury Press, 1979. Pp. 95–102.

1164 ______. "The Function of Tongues in Pentecostalism," *OC* 19:4 (1983): 332–54.

1165 ______. "Gathering the Fragments," *Wor* 33:9 (1959): 580–86.

1166 ______. "The Holy Spirit and Christian Initiation," in *The Holy Spirit and Power: The Catholic Charismatic Renewal,* Kilian McDonnel, editor. Doubleday, 1975. Pp. 101–15.

1167 ______. "Holy Spirit and Pentecostals," *Common* 89 (November 8, 1968): 198–204.

1168 ______. *Holy Spirit and Power: The Catholic Charismatic Renewal.* Doubleday, 1975.

1169 ______. "Towards a Critique of the Churches and the Charismatic Renewal," *OC* 16:4 (1980): 329–37.

1170 McDonnell, Kilian and Arnold Bittlinger. *The Baptism in the Holy Spirit as an Ecumenical Problem.* Charismatic Renewal Services, 1972.

1171 McGavran, Donald A. *Crucial Issues in Missions Tomorrow.* Moody Press, 1972.

1172 McGuire, Meredith B. "Sharing Life in the Spirit: The Function of Testimony in Catholic Pentecostal Commitment and Conversion." Paper presented at the meeting of the Society for the Scientific Study of Religion, Milwaukee, 1975.

1173 ______. "Social Context of Prophecy: 'Word-Gifts' of the Spirit Among Catholic Pentecostals," *RRelRes* 18 (Winter 1977): 134–47.

1174 ______. "Speaking of the Spirit: Language Use by Catholic Pentecostals." Unpublished report to the World Congress of Sociology, Research Committee on Sociolinguistics, 1974.

1175 McIntyre, J. "The Holy Spirit in Greek Patristic Thought," *SJT* 7 (1954): 353–75.

1176 McKenna, John H. *Eucharist and Holy Spirit: The Eucharistic Epiclesis in Twentieth-Century Theology.* Mayhew-McCrimmon, 1975.

1177 ______. "Eucharistic Epiclesis: Myopia or Microcosm," *SoThSt* 36 (June 1975): 265–84.

1178 Mackenzie, Ross. "Reformed and Roman Catholic Understandings of the Eucharist," *JES* 13 (Spring 1976): 260–66.

1179 ______. "Reformed Tradition and the Papacy," *JES* 13 (Summer 1976): 359–67.

1180 Mackenzie, William B. *The Abiding Comforter: His Person and Work.* Seeley, Jackson, and Halliday, 1859.

1181 McKeown, Robert Eugene. "A Prolegomenon to a Doctrine of the Holy Spirit: Studies in the Biblical Sources and Epistemological Considerations." Unpublished dissertation, Duke University, 1976.

1182 Mackey, C. Lloyd. "Pentecostals Proliferate Barriers," *CT* 23 (November 2, 1979): 61–63.

1183 McLaughlin, Raymond W. "The Place of the Holy Spirit in Preaching." Unpublished dissertation, Northern Baptist Seminary, 1953.

1984 McLoughlin, William G. "Is There a Third Force in Christendom?," *D* 96 (Winter 1967): 43–68.

1185 McMillan, Archibald. *The Fulness of the Spirit.* W. Kent & Co., 1870.

1186 McNair, Jim. *Experiencing the Holy Spirit: Truths That Can Transform Your Life.* Bethany Fellowship, Inc., 1977.

1187 McNamee, John J. "The Role of the Spirit in Pentecostalism: A Comparative Study." Unpublished dissertation, University of Tübingen, 1974.

1188 MacNeil, John. *The Spirit-Filled Life.* Revell Co., 1895.

1189 McPlon, James. "The Holy Spirit in Luke and John," *IrTQ* 45:2 (1978): 117–31.

1190 McTernan, J. "Water Baptism: A Response to Fr. Kilian McDonnell's Paper," *OC* 10 (1974): 203–5.

1191 Maertens, Thierry. *The Spirit of God in Scripture.* Helicon, 1966.

1192 Maginot, Norbert. *Der Actus humanus moralis unter dem Einfluss des Heiligen Geistes nach Dionysius Carthusianus.* M. Hueber, 1968.

1193 Mahan, Asa. *The Baptism of the Holy Ghost.* Edwin Newby Book Room, 1966.

1194 Mahood, John Wilmot. *Never More: The Unseen Guest—A Brief Practical Study of the Holy Spirit.* Christopher Publishing House, 1949.

1195 Makrakēs, Apostolos, with D. Cummings (trans.). *The Logos and the Holy Spirit in the Unity of Christian Thought.* 5 vols. Orthodox Christian Educational Society, 1977.

1196 Malatesta, Edward. "The Holy Spirit Accuses Us of Sin," *OC* 16:3 (1980): 195–205.

1197 ______. *Spirit of God in Christian Life.* Paulist Press, 1977.

1198 Malherbe, Abraham J. *The Holy Spirit in Athenagoras.* Clarendon Press, 1969.

1199 Malmberg, Felix J. *Eén lichaam en één geest.* N.p., 1958.

1200 Malone, Thomas P. "Christian Sacred Tradition and Psychotherapy," *OW* (1976): 26–53.

1201 Manaranche, André. *L'Esprit et la femme.* Editions du Sevil, 1974.

1202 Manning, Henry E. *The Internal Mission of the Holy Spirit.* D. & J. Sadlier & Co., 1881.

1203 ______. *The Temporal Mission of the Holy Ghost.* D. Appleton, 1866.

1204 Mansfield, M. Robert. *Spirit & Gospel in Mark.* Hendrickson Publishers, 1987.

1205 Mansure, Arthur L. "The Relation of the Paraclete to the Spiritual Presence of Jesus in the Fourth Gospel." Unpublished dissertation, Boston University, 1950.

1206 Mar, Osthathios Geevarghese Metropolitan. "Cosmic, Communitarian and Kenotic Dimensions of the New Man in Christ," *IJT* 27 (July-December 1978): 177–85.

1207 Marinelli, Francesco. "L'Incarnazione del Logos e lo Spirito Santo," *DV* 13:3 (1969): 497–555.

1208 Marmion, Columbus. *Consécration à la Sainte Trinité.* Editions de Maredsous, 1946.

1209 Marshall, I. Howard. "The Significance of Pentecost (Acts 2)," *SJT* 30:4 (1977): 347–69.

1210 Marsh, F. E. *Emblems of the Holy Spirit.* Alliance Press Company, 1911.

1211 Marsh, Thomas. "Holy Spirit in Early Christian Teaching," in *Witness to the Spirit: Essays on Revelation, Spirit, Redemption,* Wilfrid Harrington, editor. Koinonia Press, 1979. Pp. 60–78.

1212 Marston, Leslie R. "The Crisis Process Issue in Wesleyan Thought," *WTJ* 1969.

1213 Martensen, Daniel F. "Eastern Orthodoxy on Lutheran Agenda," *LW* 23:3 (1976): 166–99.

1214 Martin, Donald Nixon. "The Progressive Revelation of the Holy Spirit in the Old Testament." Unpublished dissertation, Bob Jones University, 1962.

1215 Martin, Kenneth C. "Spirit-Empowered Ministry," *BLT* 20 (Winter 1975): 45 – 51.

1216 Martin, Malcolm. "Missionary and the Holy Spirit," *M* 5 (April 1977): 223 – 39.

1217 Martin, Paul. *The Holy Spirit Today.* Beacon Hill Press, 1970.

1218 Martin, Ralph. "Baptism in the Holy Spirit: Pastoral Implications," in *The Holy Spirit and Power,* K. McDonnel, editor. Doubleday, 1975. Pp. 91 – 105.

1219 ______. (comp.). *Spirit and the Church: Personal and Documentary Record of the Charismatic Renewal, and the Ways it is Bursting to Life in the Catholic Church.* Paulist Press, 1976.

1220 Martin, Steve L. "The Doctrine of Man, Reason and the Holy Spirit in the Epistemology of Charles Hodge." Unpublished thesis, Trinity Evangelical Divinity School, 1984.

1221 Massabki, Charles. *Who Is the Holy Spirit?* Alba House, 1979.

1222 Massee, J. C. *The Holy Spirit.* Revell Co., 1940.

1223 Masterman, John H. *"I Believe in the Holy Ghost": A Study of the Doctrine of the Holy Spirit in the Light of Modern Thought.* Wells, Gardner, Darton & Co., 1909.

1224 Matheson, George. *Voices of the Spirit.* A. C. Armstrong & Son, 1910.

1225 Mathie, Rex Graham. "The Doctrine of the Holy Spirit in the Theology of Hendrikus Berkhof with Special Reference to the Relationship of the Spirit to the Father and Jesus Christ." Unpublished dissertation, University of South Africa, 1982.

1226 ______. "The Doctrine of the Holy Spirit in the Theology of Hendrikus Berkhof," *ThEv* 15:3 (December 1982): 66 – 67.

1227 Mattke, Robert A. "The Baptism of the Holy Spirit as Related to the Work of Entire Sanctification," *WTJ* (Spring 1970): 22 – 32.

1228 Maurer, Iris Sue. "Allusions to the Epistle to the Romans in 'Paradise Lost': A Comparison of Their Contexts in the Light of Reformation Theology." Unpublished dissertation, Catholic University of America, 1981.

1229 Mavis, W. Curry. *The Holy Spirit in the Christian Life.* Baker Book House,. 1977.

1230 May, F. William. "The Holy Spirit's Gift of Tongues," *Vo* 42 (October 1963): 4 – 5.

1231 Mayers, Ronald B. "Infilling of the Spirit," *RefR* 28 (Spring 1975): 157–70.

1232 Mays, Edwin J. "Paul's Teaching Concerning the Relationship of the Holy Spirit to Christian Living." Unpublished dissertation, Southwestern Baptist Seminary, 1957.

1233 Mead, Margaret. "Holy Ghost People," *AA* 70 (June 1968): 10–14.

1234 Meador, Edward Kirby. *A Diary of the Holy Spirit.* Meador Publishing Company, 1933.

1235 Meeks, M. Douglas. *God and the Economics of the Spirit.* Eden Theological Seminary, 1977.

1236 ______. "Gott und die Ökonomie des Heiligen Geistes," *EvTh* 40 (January-February 1980): 40–58.

1237 ______. "The Holy Spirit and Human Needs: Toward a Trinitarian View of Economics," *ChrCris* 40 (November 10, 1980): 307–16.

1238 Meinhold, Peter. "Les bases pneumatologiques de l'Office luthérien," in *Le Saint-Esprit dans la Liturgie,* A. Pistoia and A. Triacca, editors. Bibliotheca Ephemerides Liturgicae, 1977. Pp. 105–19.

1239 Meinhold, Theodore. *Der Heilige Geist und sein Wirken am einzelnen Menschen.* Deichert, 1890.

1240 Melotto, Angelico. "La Comunion y la Participacion en el Documento de la Tercera Conferencia General del Episcopado Latinoamericano," *EsTe* 6 (July-December 1979): 193–203.

1241 Menzies, William W. "The Methodology of Pentecostal Theology: An Essay on Hermeneutics," in *Essays on Apostolic Themes: Studies in Honor of Howard M. Ervin.* Paul Elbert, editor. Hendrickson Publishers, 1985. Pp. 1–14.

1242 Mercer, Jerry L. "The Witness of the Spirit: A Doctrine in Tension," in *The Word and the Doctrine,* Kenneth E. Geiger, editor. Beacon Hill Press, 1965. Pp. 257–70.

1243 Meskeen, Matta. "Pentecôte," *Iren* 50 (1977): 5–45.

1244 Metcalf, William. *Another Pentecost?* Challenge Books, 1973.

1245 Metz, Donald S. "The Gifts of the Spirit in Perspective," in *The Word and the Doctrine,* Kenneth E. Geiger, editor. Beacon Hill Press, 1965. Pp. 317–34.

1246 Meyendorff, John. "The Holy Spirit, as God," in *The Holy Spirit,* Dow Kirkpatrick, editor. Tidings, 1974. Pp. 76–89.

1247 Meyer, Frederick B. *The Filling of the Holy Spirit.* Revell Co., n.d.

1248 Meyer, Harding, et al., eds. *Wiederentdeckung des Heiligen Geistes: der Heilige Geist in der charismatischen Erfahrung und theologischen Reflexion.* Verlag Knecht, 1974.

1249 Meyer, Matthias. "Das 'Mutter-Amt' des Heiligen Geistes in der Theologie Zinzendorfs," *EvTh* 43 (September-October 1983): 415–30.

1250 Meyer, Paul W. "Holy Spirit in the Pauline Letters: A Contextual Exploration," *Int* 33 (January 1979): 3–18.

1251 Meynell, Hugo A. "Holy Trinity and the Corrupted Consciousness," *TH* 79 (May 1976): 143–51.

1252 Michaelis, Wilhelm. *Reich Gottes und Geist Gottes nach dem Neuen Testament.* Friedrich Reinhardt, n.d.

1253 ______. "Zur Herkunft des johanneischen Paraklet-Titels," *CN* 11 (1974): 147–62.

1254 Michaelson, Carl. "The Holy Spirit and the Church," *ThTo* 8:1 (April 1951): 41–54.

1255 Miguéns, Manuel. *El Paráclito.* Franciscan Herald Press, 1963.

1256 Miguez-Bonino, José. " 'The Spirit Groans': The Sunday Sermon," in *The Holy Spirit,* Dow Kirkpatrick, editor. Tidings, 1974. Pp. 234–39.

1257 Milavec, Aaron. "The Bible, the Holy Spirit, and Human Powers," *SJT* 29:3 (1976): 215–35.

1258 Miller, Ernest C. "The Pentecost Sermons of Lancelot Andrewes: An Ecumenical Agenda (1606–1622)," *ATR* 65 (July 1983): 306–23.

1259 Miller, Gene, Max Gaulke, and Donald Smith. *Dynamics of the Faith: Evangelical Christian Foundations.* Gulf-Coast Bible College, 1972.

1260 Miller, James Barrett. "Scripture and the English Reformation, 1526–1553." Unpublished dissertation, Fuller Theological Seminary, School of Theology, 1982.

1261 Miller, Roy L. "Beginning a Ministry of Holistic Evangelism for Youth With Local Church Members." Unpublished dissertation, Drew University, 1984.

1262 Miller, Timothy Charles. "A Study of 'Paradise Regained' in the Context of Milton's Religion of the Spirit." Unpublished dissertation, State University of New York at Binghamton, 1982.

1263 van der Minde, Hans J. "Theologia Crucis und Pneumaaussagen bei Paulus," *Cat* 34:2/3 (1980): 128–45.

1264 Minear, Paul S. "Oekumenischer Beitrag zur Pneumatologie," in *Unterwegs zur Einheit,* Johannes Brantschen and Pietro Selvatico, editors. Herder, 1980. Pp. 791–80.

1265 Mínguez, Dionisio. *Pentecostés: Ensayo de Semiótica narrativa en Hch 2.* Biblical Institute Press, 1976.

1266 Mink, Paul. *Ich bin der Herr, dein Artz! Betrachtungen über die Heilung durch den Glauben nach dem Wort Gottes.* Maranatha-Mission, n.d.

1267 Minz, Nirmal. "The Freedom of the Indigenous Church Under the Holy Spirit and Communication of the Common Christian Heritage in the Context of this Freedom," in *Gospel and Frontier Peoples,* R. Pierce Beaver, editor. William Carey Library, 1973. Pp. 96–117.

1268 Mitchell, Basil. "Traditionaliste Malgre Lui," *TH* 82 (January 1979): 31–38.

1269 Mitchell, Curtis C. "The Holy Spirit's Intercessory Ministry (Rom 8:26–27)," *BS* 139 (July-September 1982): 230–42.

1270 Mitchell, T. Crichton. "Response to Dr. Timothy Smith on the Wesleys' Hymns," *WTJ* 16 (Fall 1981): 48–57.

1271 Mitton, C. Leslie. "The Gift of the Holy Spirit (Sermon, Whitsunday; Acts 19:2)," *ExT* 63 (1952): 249–50.

1272 Moberly, George. *The Administration of the Holy Spirit in the Body of Christ.* J. Parker & Company, 1868.

1273 Moeller, Charles. "The Holy Spirit Discloses the Meaning of Creation," *OC* 16:3 (1980): 185–94.

1274 Molenaar, D. G. *De doop met de Heilige Geest.* J.H. Kok, 1963.

1275 Molland, Einar. "Den Hellige and I Oldkirkens Erfaring, Tro og Laere," *NTTid* 77:2 (1976): 87–106.

1276 Mollat, Donatien. *L'expérience de l'Esprit-Saint selon le Nouveau Testament.* Editions du Feu Nouveau, 1973.

1277 ______. *L'expérience spirituelle.* Editions du Feu Nouveau, 1974.

1278 ______. *La révélation du Saint-Esprit chez saint Jean.* Privately published, 1971.

1279 ______. "The Role of Experience in the New Testament Teaching on Baptism and the Coming of the Holy Spirit," *OC* 10 (1974): 129–47.

1280 Moller, David Wendell. "The Meaning of Dying: Values, Structure and People." Unpublished dissertation, Columbia University, 1982.

1281 Moller, F. P. "Faith and Experience," *OC* 19:4 (1983): 306–15.

1282 Moltmann, Jürgen. "Die Gemeinschaft des Heiligen Geistes: Zur Trinitarischen Pneumatologie," *ThLit* 107 (October 1982): 705–15.

1283 Moltmann, Wendel Elisabeth and Jürgen Moltmann. "Becoming Human in New Community," *CTM* 9 (October 1982): 259–70.

1284 Mondin, Battista. "The Holy Spirit as Legitimation of the Papacy," in *Conflicts about the Holy Spirit,* Hans Küng and Jürgen Moltmann, editors. Seabury Press, 1979. Pp. 63–71.

1285 Mongillo, Antonio. "Healing," in *Healing and the Spirit,* Georges Combet and Luareat Fabre, editors. Seabury Press, 1974. Pp. 124–28.

1286 Monleon, Albert Marie de. "Expérience des Charismes, Manifestations de L'Esprit en vue du Bien Commun," *Istina* 21 (October-December 1976): 340–73.

1287 Montague, George T. "Baptism in the Spirit and Speaking in Tongues: A Biblical Appraisal," *TD* 21 (1973): 342–60.

1288 ______. *The Spirit and His Gifts: The Biblical Background of Spirit-Baptism, Tongue-Speaking and Prophecy.* Paulist Press, 1974.

1289 ______. *The Holy Spirit: Growth of A Biblical Tradition.* Paulist Press, 1976.

1290 Moody, Dale. *Spirit of the Living God: The Biblical Concepts Interpreted in Context.* Westminster Press, 1968.

1291 Moody, Dwight Lyman. *Secret Power.* Revell Co., 1881.

1292 Moody, Joseph B. *Debate on Baptism and the Work of the Holy Spirit.* Brandon Company, 1889.

1293 Moore, Henry. *The Life of the Rev. John Wesley.* N. Bangs and J. Emory, 1826.

1294 Moore, John. "The Catholic Pentecostal Movement," *DL* 23 (April 1973): 177–96.

1295 Moore, Sebastian. "On Quenching the Spirit," *DR* 74:235 (Winter 1955–1956): 1–7.

1296 Mooren, Thomas. "Islam und Christentum im Horizont der anthropologischen Wirklichkeit," *ZMR* 64 (January 1980): 10–32.

1297 Moorehead, John. "The Spirit and the World," *GOTR* 26 (Spring-Summer 1981): 113–17.

1298 Morgan, G. Campbell. *The Spirit of God.* Revell Co., 1900.

1299 Morgan, James. *The Scripture Testimony of the Holy Spirit.* T. & T. Clark, 1865.

1300 Morgan, John H. "Denominational Christianity: Towards a Vindication of Pluralism," *Chm* 92:4 (1978): 331–39.

1301 Morris, John Warren. "The Charismatic Movement: An Orthodox Evaluation," *GOTR* 28 (Summer 1983): 103–34.

1302 Morris, Leon. *Spirit of the Living God.* Inter-Varsity Fellowship, 1960.

1303 Moule, C. F. D. *The Holy Spirit.* Mowbrays, 1978.

1304 Moule, Handley C. G. *Veni Creator: Thoughts on the Person and Work of the Holy Spirit of Promise.* T. Whittaker, 1890.

1305 Mowinckel, Sigmund. "Die Vorstellungen des Späjudentums vom Heiligen Geist als Fürsprecher und der johanneische Paraklete," *ZNW* 32 (1933): 97–130.

1306 Moozoomdar, Protap Chunder. *The Spirit of God.* G. H. Ellis, 1894.

1307 Mühlen, Heribert. "Der Aufbruch einer neuen Verehrung Marias," *Cat* 29:2–3 (1975): 145–63.

1308 ______. *A Catholic Theology.* Burns, Oates & Washbourne, 1978.

1309 ______. *A Charismatic Theology.* Paulist Press, 1978.

1310 ______. *Erfahrung mit dem Heiligen Geist.* Grünewald Verlag, 1979.

1311 ______. "Der gegenwärtige Aufbruch der Geisterfahrung und die Unterscheidung der Geister," in *Gegenwart des Geistes: Aspekte der Pneumatologie,* Walter Kasper, editor. Herder, 1979. Pp. 24–53.

1312 ______. *Der Heilige Geist als Person.* Aschendorff, 1963.

1313 ______. "Das Pneuma Jesu und die Zeit," *Cat* 17 (1963): 249–76.

1314 Mullen, Laurence K. "Holy Living: The Adequate Ethic," *WTJ* 14 (Fall 1979): 82–95.

1315 Müller-Schwefe, Hans R. *Der Geist macht lebendig.* Agentur des Rauhen Hauses, 1970.

1316 Mumaw, John R. "The Holy Spirit at Work as Predicted in the Gospel of John," in *Encounter with the Holy Spirit,* George R. Brunk, II, editor. Herald Press, 1972. Pp. 189–21.

1317 Munchinsky, George. "The Harmonious Use of the Gifts of the Holy Spirit." Unpublished dissertation, Bethel Seminary, 1981.

1318 Munnell, T. "The Holy Spirit in Consciousness," in *A Symposium on the Holy Spirit*. John Burns, 1879. Pp. 79–101.

1319 Munro, John K. "The New Testament Spiritual Gifts." Unpublished master's thesis, Dallas Theological Seminary, 1940.

1320 Murphy, Henry. "The Indwelling of Christ in Man." Unpublished dissertation, Catholic University of America, 1972.

1321 Murray, Andrew. *Back to Pentecost*. Oliphants, n.d.

1322 ______. *The One Thing Needful: The Full Blessing of Pentecost*. Oliphants, 1944.

1323 ______. *Spirit of Christ*. James Nisbet & Company, 1888.

1324 Murray, Jurretta J. "The Relationship of the Spirit in the Earlier Paulines and in Matthew." Unpublished dissertation, Boston University, 1940.

1325 Murray, Pauli. "The Holy Spirit and God Language," *Wit* 66:2 (Fall 1983): 7–9.

1326 Murray, Robert. "New Wine in Old Wineskins, XII: Firstfruits," *ExT* 86 (March 1975): 164–68.

1327 Mussner, F. "Die johanneische Parakletsprüche und die Apostolische Tradition," *BibZ* 5 (1961): 56–70.

1328 Myers, Cortland. *The Real Holy Spirit*. Revell Co., 1909.

N

1329 Napiorkowski, Stanislaw C., with H. d'Anjou (trans.). "Christus Solus Numquam Solus: Toward Reinterpretation of the Principle 'Solus Christus,' " *JES* 17 (Summer 1980): 454–76.

1330 Nautin, Pierre. *Je crois à l'Esprit Saint dans la Sainte Eglise pour la Résurrection de la chair.* Les Editions du Cerf, 1947.

1331 Nebe, Otto H. *Deus spiritus sanctus: Untersuchungen zur Lehre vom Heiligen Geist.* C. Bertelsmann, 1939.

1332 Neff, H. Richard. "The Cultural Basis for Glossolalia in the Twentieth Century," in *Speaking in Tongues: Let's Talk About It,* Watson E. Mills, editor. Word Books, 1973. Pp. 26–35.

1333 Neitz, Mary J. "Slain in the Spirit: Creating and Maintaining a Religious Social Reality," *RelEd* 78 (Summer 1983): 423–24.

1334 Nelson, C. Ellis. "Habitat of the Spirit," *PSB* NS 1:3 (1977): 111–16.

1335 Nelson, J. Robert. "Arrivederci, Pneuma (Special Report: International Theological Congress on Pneumatology, Rome, MR 1982)," *ChrCent* 99 (June 2, 1982): 667–69.

1336 ______. "Christian Ministry and Sacraments: A Comment on the Cocu Ministry Statement," *QR* 1 (Spring 1981): 86–93.

1337 ______. "The Holy Spirit: Personal, Ecclesial, Mundane," *RL* 48 (Summer 1979): 203–16.

1338 ______. "International Theological Congress on Pneumatology (Rome, MR 1982; rpt.)," *JES* 19 (Summer 1982): 675–78.

1339 Ness, Henry H. *The Baptism with the Holy Spirit: What Is It?* Evangelism Crusaders, Inc., n.d.

1340 ______. *Manifestations of the Spirit.* Privately published, n.d.

1341 Neunheuser, Burkhard. "Taufe im Geist: Der Heilige Geist in den Riten der Taufliturgie," in *Archiv für Liturgiewissenschaft, Band 12,* Emmanuel von Severus, editor. Pustet, 1970. Pp. 268–84.

1342 ______. "Taufe im Geist: Der Heilige Geist in den Riten der Taufliturgie," in *Le Saint-Esprit dans la Liturgie,* A. Pistoia and A. Triacca, editors. Bibliotheca Ephemerides Liturgicae, 1977. Pp. 121–40.

1343 Neve, Lloyd. *The Spirit of God in The Old Testament.* Seibunsha, 1972.

1344 Neville, Robert. "The Holy Spirit as God," in *Is God God?* Axel Steuer and James W. McClendon, editors. Abingdon Press, 1981. Pp. 235–64.

1345 Newbigin, Lesslie. *The Holy Spirit and the Church.* Christian Literature Society, 1972.

1346 ______. "Témoins du Royaume: L'Eglise," *Flam* 55 (March 1979): 276–80.

1347 Newell, Arlo F. *Receive the Holy Spirit.* Warner Press, 1978.

1348 Newman, Paul W. "Humanity with Spirit," *SJT* 34 (1981): 415–26.

1349 Nicholson, Roy S. *The Arminian Emphasis.* N.p., n.d.

1350 Nicklasson, Gosta. "Spiritual Renewal," in *Vocation and Victory (Salvation Army),* Jurgen W. Winterhager, editor. Brunnen Publishing House, 1970. Pp. 297–30.

1351 Niederwimmer, Kurt, et al., eds. *Unterscheidung der Geister.* Johannes Stauda Verlag, 1972.

1352 Niesel, Wilhelm. "Das Zeugnis von der Kraft des Heiligen Geistes im Heidelberger Katechismus," in *Warum wirst du ein Christ Genannt,* Walter Herrnbrüch and Udo Smith, editors. Neukirchener Verlag, 1965. Pp. 79–93.

1353 Nissiotis, Nikos A. "Called to Unity: The Significance of the Invocation of the Spirit for Church Unity," in *Lausanne 77: Fifty Years of Faith,* Lucas Vischer, et al., editors. N.p., 1977. Pp. 48–64.

1354 ______. "Der Pneumatologische Ansatz und die Liturgische Verwirklichung des Neutestamentlichen Nyn," in *Oikonomia: Heilsgeschichte. Oscar Cullmann zum 65 Geburtstag,* Fely Christ, editor. Herbert Reich Evangelische Verlag, 1967. Pp. 302–30.

1355 ______. "Pneumatological Christology as a Presupposition of Ecclesiology," in *Oecumenica: An Annual Symposium of Ecumenical Research.* Frederich W. Kantzenbach, editor. 1967. Pp. 235–50.

1356 Noble, David A. "The Holy Spirit in the Johannine Writings." Unpublished dissertation, Southern Baptist Seminary, 1938.

1357 Noll, Mark A. "John Wesley and the Doctrine of Assurance," *BS* 132 (April-June 1975): 161–77.

1358 Nordhues, Paul and Heinrich Petri. *Die Gabe Gottes: Beiträge zur Theologie und Pastoral des Firmsakramentes.* Bonifacius-Druckerei, 1974.

1359 Northrup, Bernard E. *What You Should Know About . . . Tongues and Spiritual Gifts.* San Francisco Baptist Seminary, n.d.

1360 Nösgen, Karl F. *Geschichte der Lehre vom Heiligen Geiste.* C. Bertelsmann, 1899.

1361 Nossol, Alfons. "Der Geist als Gegenwart Jesu Christi," in *Gegenwart des Geistes: Aspekte der Pneumatologie,* Walter Kasper, editor. Herder, 1979. Pp. 132–54.

1362 Nuttall, Geoffrey F. *The Holy Spirit and Ourselves.* Epworth, 1966.

1363 ______. *The Holy Spirit in Puritan Faith and Experience.* Basil Blackwell, 1946.

O

1364 Oates, Wayne E. *The Holy Spirit and Contemporary Man.* Baker Book House, 1974.

1365 ______. "The Holy Spirit and the Overseer of the Flock," *RE* 63:2 (Spring 1966): 187–97.

1366 ______. *The Holy Spirit in Five Worlds: The Psychedelic, the Non-Verbal, the Articulate, the New Morality, the Administrative.* Association Press, 1968.

1367 Oberholzer, Felicidad. "The Transformation of Evil into Sin and Sin into Sorrow and Forgiveness: Lessons from Analytic Psychology and Theology." Unpublished dissertation, Graduate Theological Union, 1984.

1368 O'Brien, Regina Jean Maria. "An Experiment in Preparation for Ministry: Power and Its Implications for Ministry." Unpublished dissertation, Drew University, 1980.

1369 Ockenga, Harold J. *The Holy Spirit and Tongues.* Boston Park Street Church, 1965.

1370 ______. *Power Through Pentecost.* Eerdmans Publishing Co., 1959.

1371 ______. *The Spirit of the Living God.* Revell Co., 1947.

1372 O'Connor, Edward D. "Baptism of the Spirit: Emotional Therapy?" *AveM* 106 (1967): 11–14.

1373 ______. "The Hidden Roots of the Charismatic Renewal in the Catholic Church," in *Aspects of Pentecostal-Charismatic Origins,* Vinson Synan, editor. Logos International, 1975. Pp. 169–91.

1374 ______. "The Holy Spirit, Christian Love, and Mysticism," in *Perspectives on Charismatic Renewal,* Edward D. O'Connor, editor. University of Notre Dame Press, 1975. Pp. 133–44.

1375 ______, ed. *Perspectives on Charismatic Renewal.* University of Notre Dame Press, 1975.

1376 O'Driscoll, Joseph A. *The Holy Spirit and the Art of Living.* B. Herder Book Co., 1959.

1377 Oeyen, Christian. "Die Lehre der Göttlichen Kräfte bei Justin," in *Studia Patristica,* Frank Cross, editor. Akademie Verlag, 1972. Pp. 215–21.

1378 Office of the General Assembly. *The World of the Holy Spirit.* United Presbyterian Church USA, 1970.

1379 Oglesby, Stuart Roscoe. *You and the Holy Spirit: A Neglected New Testament Doctrine Made Personal and Practical for Everyday Life.* John Knox Press, 1952.

1380 Okulu, Henry J., et al., eds. *Facing the New Challenges: The Message of Paul.* Evangel Publishing House, 1978.

1381 Oliver, Albert Benjamin. *The Person and Work of the Holy Spirit.* Casa Publicadona Batista, n.d.

1382 Olson, Roger Eugene. "Trinity and Eschatology: The Historical Being of God in the Theology of Wolfhart Pannenberg." Unpublished dissertation, Rice University, 1984.

1383 O'Neill, J. C. "The Unforgivable Sin (Matt 12:31–32; Mark 3:28f; Luke 12:10)," *JSNT* 19 (1983): 37–42.

1384 Onerton, John H. *The Evangelical Revival in the Eighteenth Century.* Longmans, Green & Co., 1900.

1385 ______. *John Wesley.* Methuen & Company, 1891.

1386 Onibere, S. G. A. Ose. "The Phenomenon of African Religious Independency: Blessing or Curse on the Church Universal," *ATJ* 10:1 (1981): 9–26.

1387 Oomen, Christian. *Het Bijbelgetuigenis over Christus den levengevenden geest.* de Kinkhoren, 1946.

1388 Oosterman, John Bernard. "Peter Daimani's Doctrine on the Sacerdotal Office: A Canonical Study of the Validity of Orders and the Worthy Exercise of Ordained Ministry." Unpublished dissertation, Catholic University of America, 1980.

1389 Oosthuizen, Gerhardus C. "Misunderstanding of the Holy Spirit in the Independent Movements in Africa," in *Christusprediking in de Wereld: J. H. Bavinck,* A. Pos, et al., editors. J. H. Kok, 1965. Pp. 78–89.

1390 Opsahl, Paul D., ed. *The Holy Spirit in the Life of the Church: From Biblical Times to the Present.* Augsburg Publishing Co., 1978.

1391 Orbe, Antonio. *La teologia del Expiritu Santo.* Libreria Editrice dell'Universitá Gregoriana, 1966.

1392 ______. "Los Valentianos y el Matrimonio Espiritual: Hacia los Origenes de la Mistica Nupcial," *Greg* 58:1 (1977): 5–53.

1393 O'Reilly, K. "The Roman Catholic Magisterium and Legitimate Dissent," in *Authority, Conscience and Dissent,* B. P. Ashby, et al., editors. Paulist Press, 1971. Pp. 124–46.

1394 Osburn, Carroll D. "The Interpretation of Romans 8:28," *WTJ* 44 (Spring 1982): 99–109.

1395 Osgood, DeWitt S. *Preparing for the Latter Rain.* Southern Publishing Association, 1973.

1396 Osteen, John H. "He Heard God Speak," *BBHS* (1963): 6–10.

1397 Osten, Sacken Peter von der. "Geist im Buchstaben: Vom Glanz des Mose und des Paulus," *EvTh* 41 (May-June 1981): 230–35.

1398 Osterhaven, M. Eugene. "Calvin on the Covenant," *RefR* 33 (Spring 1980): 136–49.

1399 ______. "John Calvin: Order and the Holy Spirit," *RefR* 32 (Fall 1978): 23–44.

1400 ______. "Studies in Calvin," *RefR* 32 (Fall 1978): 4–44.

1401 Oswalt, John N. "John Wesley and the Old Testament Concept of the Holy Spirit," *RL* 48 (Autumn 1979): 283–92.

1402 Otis, George. *God the Holy Spirit.* Bible Voice Books, 1970.

1403 O'Toole, Robert F. "Activity of the Risen Jesus in Luke–Acts," *Bib* 62:4 (1981): 471–98.

1404 Otterness, Omar. "Holy Spirit and the People of God in the Theology of Joseph Haroutunian," *PSB* NS 1:1 (1977): 68–75.

1405 Ott, Heinrich. "Heiliger Geist und säkulare Wirklichkeit," *ThZ* 33 (September-October 1977): 336–45.

1406 Otto, Rudolf. *Die Anschauung vom Heiligen Geiste bei Luther.* Vandenhoeck & Ruprecht, 1898.

1407 ______. *Geist und Wort nach Luther.* Huth, 1898.

1408 Oudersluys, Richard C. "The Purpose of Spiritual Gifts," *RefR* 28 (Spring 1975): 212–22.

1409 Oulton, John E. L. *Holy Communion and Holy Spirit.* SPCK, 1954.

1410 Owen, John. *The Holy Spirit.* Kregel, 1960.

1411 Owen, John R. *On the Holy Spirit.* 2 vols. Protestant Episcopal Book Society, 1862.

P

1412 Pache, René, with J. D. Emerson (trans.). *The Person and Work of the Holy Spirit.* Moody Press, 1954.

1413 Packer, James. "The Holy Spirit in the Corporate Life of the Pauline Congregation." Unpublished dissertation, Concordia Seminary, 1974.

1414 ______. *Keep in Step with the Spirit.* Revell Co., 1984.

1415 Padilla, C. René. *New Face of Evangelism: An International Symposium on the Lausanne Covenant.* Hodder & Stoughton, 1976.

1416 Pagard, Kenneth. "Fellowship of the Holy Spirit," in *Jesus, Where are You Taking Us? Messages from the First International Lutheran Conference on the Holy Spirit,* Norris L. Wogen, editor. Creation House, 1973. Pp. 135–65.

1417 Palachkovsky, Vsévolod. "Les 'Pneumatica' des antiphones graduelles," in *Le Saint-Esprit dans la Liturgie,* A. Pistoia and A. Triacca, editors. Bibliotheca Ephemerides Liturgicae, 1977. Pp. 141–48.

1418 Palma, Anthony D. "The Holy Spirit in the Corporate Life of the Pauline Congregation." Unpublished dissertation, Concordia Seminary, 1974.

1419 ______. *The Spirit: God in Action.* Gospel Publishing House, 1974.

1420 Palmer, Edwin H. *The Holy Spirit.* Presbyterian and Reformed Publishing Company, 1962.

1421 ______. *Person and Ministry of the Holy Spirit: The Traditional Calvinistic Perspective.* Baker Book House, 1974.

1422 Papa, Mary. "Pentecostals: Wave of the Future," *NCR* 4 (June 5, 1969): 1–2.

1423 Papadakis, Aristeides. "Gregory II of Cyrus and Mark's Report Again," *GOTR* 21 (Summer 1976): 147–57.

1424 Papandreou, Damaskinos Metr of Tranoupolis. "The Holy Spirit in the Church," *Diak* 17:1 (1982): 40–45.

1425 Paprocki, Henry K. "Le Saint Esprit dans les Sacrements de l'Eglise (Eucharist)," *Istina* 28 (July-September 1983): 267–81.

1426 Parcher, Kimberly S. "John 14:17 and the Indwelling/Enablement Debate." Unpublished dissertation, Grace Theological Seminary, 1984.

1427 Pardington, George Palmer. "Spirit Incarnate: The Doctrine of the Holy Spirit in Relation to Process Philosophy." Unpublished dissertation, Graduate Theological Union, 1972.

1428 ______. "Theology and Spiritual Renewal: Methodological Reflections on a Foundational Theology of the Spirit," *ATR* 64 (April 1982): 163–79.

1429 Parent, Rémi. *L'Esprit Saint et la Liberté*. Le Centurion, 1976.

1430 Parker, Joseph. *The Paraclete: An Essay on the Personality and Ministry of the Holy Ghost*. Scribner's, 1875.

1431 Parker, Lois Wilson. "The Muse of 'Paradise Lost'; The Holy Spirit." Unpublished dissertation, Southern Illinois University at Carbondale, 1970.

1432 Parker, Pierson. "How They Looked at Jesus," *SLJ* 19 (December 1975): 67–77.

1433 Parmer, Phill Warren. " 'Like Little Paul in Person, Voice, and Grace': A Comparative Study of Edward Taylor and St. Paul." Unpublished dissertation, Louisiana State University and Agricultural and Mechanical College, 1981.

1434 Parratt, J. K. "The Rebaptism of the Ephesian Disciples," *ExT* 79 (June 1968): 182–83.

1435 Parsons, Donald J. "Some Theological and Pastoral Implications of Confirmation," in *Confirmation Re-Examined,* Kendig B. Cully, editor. Moorehouse-Marlow, 1982. Pp. 45–59.

1436 Parys, Michel van. "Lettre de Saint Arsene," *Iren* 54:1 (1981): 62–86.

1437 Patacsi, Gabriel. "Palamism Before Palamas," *EChR* 9:1–2 (1977): 64–71.

1438 Patrick, James. "Baptism, Unity, and the Ecumenical History of Grace: The Holy Spirit in Individuals and the Church," *MSt* 22 (July 1981): 228–42.

1439 Patterson, Bob E. "Catholic Pentecostals," in *Speaking in Tongues: Let's Talk About It,* Watson E. Mills, editor. Word Books, 1973. Pp. 94–111.

1440 Patterson, John W. "A Comparative Study of the Holy Spirit in the Gospels." Unpublished dissertation, Southwestern Baptist Seminary, 1955.

1441 Paulsen, Jan. *When the Spirit Descends.* Review and Herald Publishing Association, 1977.

1442 Pawelitzki, Richard. "Zeitgeist und Heiliger Geist," *ZRGG* 29:2 (1977): 97–104.

1443 Paxson, Ruth. *The Work of God the Holy Spirit.* Moody Press, 1958.

1444 Payne, Leanne. *Real Presence: The Holy Spirit in the Works of C. S. Lewis.* Cornerstone Books, 1979.

1445 Pearlman, Myer. *The Heavenly Gift: Studies in the Work of the Holy Spirit.* Gospel Publishing House, 1935.

1446 Peck, George B. *Steps and Studies: An Inquiry concerning the Gift of the Holy Spirit.* Watchword Publications, 1890.

1447 Peck, John. *What the Bible Teaches Us About the Holy Spirit.* Tyndale, 1979.

1448 Peelman, Achiel. "L'Esprit et Marie dans L'Oeuvre Theologique de Hans Urs von Balthasar," *SEs* 30 (October-December 1978): 279–94.

1449 Peiter, Hermann. "Gesetz und Evangelium als Interpretament der Sog Vernunft des Glaubens," *KD* 30 (January-March 1984): 41–70.

1450 Pelikan, Jaroslav. "The 'Spiritual Sense' of Scripture: The Exegetical Basis for St. Basil's Doctrine of the Holy Spirit," in *Basil of Caesarea,* Paul J. Fedwick, editor. Pontifical Institute for Medieval Studies, 1981. Pp. 337–60.

1451 Pelletier, Joseph. *A New Pentecost: Renewal in the Holy Spirit.* Assumption Publications, 1973.

1452 Pennington, Basil and Francis Sullivan. "Baptism in the Holy Spirit and Christian Tradition," in *Spirit and the Church,* Ralph Martin, compiler. Pentecostal Publishing House, 1977. Pp. 192–98.

1453 Pennington, John E. "The Relationship of the Human Spirit to the Holy Spirit in the Process of Healing," in *Healing and Religious Faith,* Claude A. Frazier, editor. Pilgrim Press, 1974. Pp. 153–63.

1454 Perkins, Jonathan E. *The Baptism of the Holy Spirit: An Explanation of Speaking in Other Languages as the Spirit Giveth Utterance.* B. N. Robertson, 1945.

1455 Perkins, Pheme. " 'An Ailment of Childhood': Spiritual Pediatrics for Adults (Phil 2:6–11; Rom 8; 1 Cor 15)," in *Dimensions of Contemporary Spirituality,* Francis A. Eigo, editor. Villanova University Press, 1982. Pp. 79–115.

1456 "The Person and Work of the Holy Spirit, with Special Reference to 'The Baptism in the Holy Spirit.' " Report to the Presbyterian Church in the U.S., submitted to the General Assembly, 1971.

1457 "The Person and Work of the Holy Spirit: With Special Reference to 'The Baptism of the Holy Spirit,' " in *Church Studies on the Holy Spirit,* Marvin Simmers, editor. John Knox Press, 1983. Pp. 8–28.

1458 Persson, Per Erik. "Das Amt des Geistes," *KD* 5 (April 1959): 99–116.

1459 Peterson, Edward Derel. "The Deacon in Perspective: An Experiment in the Training of Deacons at the First Assembly of God, Westminster, Maryland." Unpublished dissertation, Drew University, 1982.

1460 Peterson, Ingrid Janet. "William of Nassington: Canon, Mystic, and Poet of the 'Speculum Vitae.' " Unpublished dissertation, University of Iowa, 1982.

1461 Peterson, Robert Arthur. "Calvin's Doctrine of the Atonement." Unpublished dissertation, Drew University, 1980.

1462 Petras, David M. "The Liturgical Theology of Marriage (Byzantine Church)," *Diak* 16:3 (1981): 225–37.

1463 Petrelli, Giuseppe. *Heavenword: Book 1, the Holy Spirit.* Van Rees Press, 1953.

1464 Peyrot, Lucien. *Le Saint-Esprit et le prochain retrouvé.* Labor et Fides, 1974.

1465 Pfister, Willibald. *Das Leben im Geist nach Paulus.* Universitätsverlag, 1963.

1466 Pfitzner, Victor C. *Led in the Spirit.* Lutheran Publishing House, 1976.

1467 ______. " 'Pneumatic' Apostleship: Apostle and Spirit in the Acts of the Apostles," in *Wort in der Zeit,* Wilfrid Haubeck, editor. E. J. Brill, 1980. Pp. 210–35.

1468 Phelps, Austin. *The New Birth: The Work of the Holy Spirit.* Gould, Kendall, and Lincoln, 1867.

1469 Philibert, Paul J. "Theological Guidance for Moral Development Research," in *Essays in Morality and Ethics,* James Gaffney, editor. Paulist Press, 1980. Pp. 106–25.

1470 Philip, Abraham. "Mobilization of the Laity in the Mar Thoma Church for Evangelism." Unpublished dissertation, Fuller Theological Seminary, 1974.

1471 Philip, Marie. "Christ, Candlestick of Three Tabernacles," *OF* 24 (1949–1950): 542–52.

1472 Philip, Robert. *The Love of the Spirit.* Ward & Company, 1836.

1473 Pickard, Howard Edwin. "Paul's Conception of the Holy Spirit with Special Reference to His Ministry to the Churches." Unpublished thesis, Princeton University, 1947.

1474 Pickford, J.H. *This Is Not That: What Is the Baptism of the Holy Spirit?* N.p., 1953.

1475 Pierce, Samuel Eyles. *The Gospel of the Spirit.* Eerdmans Publishing Co., 1955.

1476 Pierson, Arthur T. *Acts of the Holy Spirit.* Revell Co., 1896.

1477 Pieters, André. "The Spirit of God and the Human Spirit," in *The Holy Spirit,* Dow Kirkpatrick, editor. Tidings, 1974. Pp. 105–24.

1478 Pink, Arthur W. *The Holy Spirit.* Baker Book House, 1970.

1479 Piper, John. "Jonathan Edwards on the Problem of Faith and History," *SJT* 31:3 (1978): 217–28.

1480 Piper, Otto. *The Holy Spirit: A Seminar on the Person and Work of the Holy Spirit.* Mimeographed paper, Princeton Theological Seminary, 1960.

1481 Pistoia, A. and A. M. Triacca, eds. *Le Saint-Esprit dans la liturgie: Conferences Saint-Serge XVIE Semaine d'Etudes Liturgiques, Paris, 1969.* Edizioni Liturgiche, 1977.

1482 Pittenger, William Norman. *The Holy Spirit.* Pilgrim Press, 1974.

1483 Pitzer, Alexander W. *The Manifold Ministry of the Holy Spirit.* Presbyterian Board of Publication, 1894.

1484 Plathow, Michael. Geist und Gebet.*KD* 29 (January-March 1983): 47–65.

1485 Platt, Frederic. *The Theology of the "Warmed Heart."* Epworth, 1938.

1486 Ploeger, Henk. *Der Heilige Geist: die uns fordernde macht.* N.p., n.d.

1487 Poinsenet, Marie D. *Je vous enverrai l'Esprit-Saint.* Desclée, 1975.

1488 Poloma, Margaret M. *The Charismatic Movement: Is There a New Pentecost?* Twayne, 1982.

1489 Pomerville, Paul Anthony. *The Third Force in Missions. A Pentecostal Contribution to Contemporary Mission Theology.* Hendrickson, 1985.

1490 Pope, R. Martin. "The Holy Spirit," *LTQ* 15 (July 1980): 82–96.

1491 Porsch, Felix. *Pneuma und Wort.* Verlag Knecht, 1974.

1492 de la Potterie, Ignace. "Chrétien Conduit par l'Esprit dans sons Cheminement Eschatologique (Rom 8:14)," in *The Law of the Spirit in Romans 7 and 8,* Lorenzo de Lorenzi, editor. N.p. 1976. Pp. 19–46.

1493 ______. "La Mort du Christ d'après Saint Jean," *StMiss* 31 (1982): 19–36.

1494 la Potterie, Ignace de and Stanislas Lyonnet. *The Christian Lives by the Spirit.* Alba House, 1970.

1495 Pou Ruis, Ramon. "L'Esglesia Cristiana, que Testimonia," in *Transcendencia I Testimoniatge,* J. M. Rovira Belloso, et al., editors. Facultat de Theologia de Barcelona, 1977. Pp. 79–104.

1496 Powell, Sidney Waterbury. *Fire on the Earth.* Broadman Press, 1963.

1497 Pratt, Samuel W. *The Gospel of the Holy Spirit.* Anson D. F. Randolph & Co., 1892.

1498 Preiss, Théodore M. *Das innere Zeugnis des Heiligen Geistes.* Evangelisches Verlag, 1947.

1499 ______. *Le Témoignage intérieur du Saint-Esprit.* Delachaux & Niestlé, 1946.

1500 Prenter, Regin. *Le Saint-Esprit et le renouveau de l'église.* Delachaux & Niestlé, 1949.

1501 ______. *Spiritus Creator: Luther's Concept of the Holy Spirit.* Muhlenberg Press, 1953.

1502 Preston, Thomas S. *The Divine Paraclete.* Robert Coddington, 1879.

1503 Pretlove, John Lionell. "Baptism 'en Pneumati'; A Comparison of the Theologies of Luke and Paul." Unpublished dissertation, Southwestern Baptist Seminary, 1980.

1504 Preus, James S. "Theological Legitimation for Innovation in the Middle Ages," in *Viator,* Lynn White, editor. University of California Press, 1972. 3:1–26.

1505 Price, Robert M. "The Centrality and Scope of Conversion," *JPTh* 9 (Spring 1981): 26–36.

1506 Prince, Michael Lee. "A Small Group Study of the Holy Spirit." Unpublished dissertation, Southwestern Baptist Seminary, 1978.

1507 Principe, Walter H. "Odo Rigaldi, A Precursor of St. Bonaventure on the Holy Spirit as Effectus Formalis in the Mutual Love of the Father and Son," in *Mediaeval Studies,* V. Brown, editor. N.p., 1977. Pp. 130–45.

1508 Pro, Mundi Vita. "Catholic Pentecostal Movement: Creative or Divisive Enthusiasm," *PMV* 60 (May 1976): 3–36.

1509 Provence, Thomas Edward. "The Hermeneutics of Karl Barth." Unpublished dissertation, Fuller Theological Seminary, 1980.

1510 Pruett, Gordon E. "Protestant Doctrine of the Eucharistic Presence," *CTJ* 10 (November 1975): 142–74.

1511 Pytches, David. "The Spirit and Evangelism," in *Bishop's Move,* Michael Harper, editor. Hodder & Stoughton, 1978. Pp. 61–76.

1512 Quanbeck, Warren A. "Developmental Perspective and the Doctrine of the Spirit," in *The Holy Spirit in the Life of the Church: From Biblical Times to the Present,* Paul D. Opsahl, editor. Augsburg Publishing Co., 1978. Pp. 158–71.

1513 Queralt, Antonio. "Christ the Lord and the Holy Spirit," in *The Spirit of God in Christian Life,* Edward Malatesta, editor. Paulist Press, 1977. Pp. 98–147.

1514 Quere, Ralph W. "The Spirit and the Gifts Are Ours: Imparting or Imploring the Spirit in Ordination Rites," *LQ* 27 (November 1975): 322–46.

1515 Quick, Tamara M. "Personal Revelation," in *Blueprints for Living,* M. Mouritsen, editor. N.p., 1980. Pp. 230–43.

1516 Quinn, Jerome D. "The Holy Spirit in the Pastoral Epistles," in *Sin, Salvation, and the Spirit,* D. Durken, editor. Revell Co., 1979. Pp. 121–34.

1517 ______. "Ordination in the Pastoral Epistles," *Com* 8 (Winter 1981): 358–69.

1518 Quispel, Gilles. "Genius and Spirit," in *Essays on the Nag Hammadi Texts,* Martin Krause, editor. E. J. Brill, 1975. Pp. 155–69.

1519 ______. "De Heilige Geest volgens de Oude Kerk," in *De Spiritu Sancto.* Kemick, 1964. Pp. 76–88.

1520 Quistorp, H. J. J. "Calvins Lehre vom Heiligen Geist," in *De Spiritu Sancto.* Kemick, 1964. Pp. 109–15.

R

1521 Rade, Martin. *Glaubenslehre.* F. A. Perthes, 1924.

1522 Radl, Walter. " 'Firmung' im Neuen Testament," *IKZ* 11 (September 1982): 427–33.

1523 Ragaz, Leonhard. *Der Paraclet.* W. Imbaumgarten, 1945.

1524 Rahner, Karl. "Ervaring van de Geest en existentiële beslissing," in *Leven uit de geest.* Hilversum, 1974. Pp. 150–61.

1525 ______. "Experience of the Spirit and Existential Decision," in *Experience of the Spirit,* edited by Peter Huizing and William Bassett. Seabury Press, 1974. Pp. 38–46.

1526 ______. *Spirit in the Church.* Seabury Press, 1979.

1527 ______. *Spirit in the World.* Sheed & Ward, 1968.

1528 Raitt, Jill. "Three Inter-Related Principles in Calvin's Unique Doctrine of Infant Baptism," *SCJ* 11:1 (1980): 51–61.

1529 Ramay, Marion Edgar. *The Work of the Holy Spirit.* Oklahoma Baptist University Press, 1953.

1530 Rambaldi, Giuseppe. "Uso e Significato di Carisma nel Vaticano II: Analisi e Confronto di Due Passi Conciliari Sui Carismi," *Greg* 56:1 (1975): 141–62.

1531 Ramm, Bernard. *Rapping about the Spirit.* Word Books, 1974.

1532 ______. *The Witness of the Spirit.* Eerdmans Publishing Co., 1960.

1533 Ramsey, Arthur M. *Holy Spirit: A Biblical Study.* SPCK, 1977.

1534 Ramsey, Arthur M., et al., eds. "Life in the Spirit." Lectures read at a conference for Anglican Religious at St. John's College, York, England, July 1974.

1535 Ramsey, Arthur M., et al., eds. *The Charismatic Christ.* Morehouse-Barlow, 1973.

1536 Ramsey, Ian Thomas. *Models for Divine Activity.* SCM Press, 1973.

1537 Rand, Cuthbert. "The Holy Spirit Transforms Us into a New Creation in Christ and Thereby Incorporates Us into the Christian Community," *OC* 16:3 (1980): 208–13.

1538 Rasco, Emilio. "Jesus y el Espiritu, Iglesia e Historia: Elementos Para Una Lectura de Lucas," *Greg* 56:2 (1975): 321–68.

1539 Rattenburg, J. Ernest. *The Conversion of the Wesleys: A Critical Study.* Epworth, 1938.

1540 Ratzinger, Joseph Cardinal. "Die kirchliche Lehre vom Sacramentum Ordinis," *IKZ* 10 (September 1981): 435–45.

1541 Raven, Charles E. *The Creator Spirit.* Harvard University Press, 1928.

1542 Rayan, Samuel. *The Holy Spirit: Heart of the Gospel and Christian Hope.* Orbis Books, 1978.

1543 Rea, John. "The Personal Relationship of Old Testament Believers to the Holy Spirit," in *Essays on Apostolic Themes: Studies in Honor of Howard M. Ervin.* Paul Elbert, editor. Hendrickson Publishers, 1985. Pp. 92–103.

1544 Read, D. H. C. "The Spirit Giveth Life (Sermon, Whitsunday; 2 Cor 3:5–6)," *ExT* 64 (1953): 247–48.

1545 Reece, T. *The Holy Spirit.* N.p., 1914.

1546 Reed, Charles Michael. "A Teacher's Manual for the Presentation of the Biblical Material on the Gifts of the Holy Spirit." Unpublished dissertation, Western Conservative Baptist Seminary, 1981.

1547 Rees, R. Montgomery. *Aspects of the Doctrine of the Holy Spirit.* Epworth Press, 1920.

1548 Rees, Thomas. *The Holy Spirit in Thought and Experience.* Scribner's, 1915.

1549 ______. *The Spirit of Life.* Hildenborough Hall, 1954.

1550 Reeves, Marjorie E. "The Originality and Influence of Joachim of Fiore," *Tra* 36 (1980): 269–316.

1551 Regan, Patrick. "Pneumatological and Eschatological Aspects of Liturgical Celebration," *Wor* 51 (July 1977): 332–50.

1552 Reiling, Jannes. *The New Testament Doctrine of the Holy Spirit.* N.p., n.d.

1553 Reinhard, Wilhelm. *Das Wirken des Heiligen Geistes im Menschen nach den Briefen des Apostels Paulus.* Herder, 1918.

1554 Renoux, Athanase. "L'Office de la Génuflexion dans la tradition arménienne," in *Le Saint-Esprit dans la Liturgie,* A. Pistoia and A. Triacca, editors. Bibliotheca Ephemerides Liturgicae, 1977. Pp. 149–63.

1555 "Report of the Consultation of the Significance of the Charismatic Renewal for the Churches, Bossey, 8–13 March 1980," *OC* 16:4 (1980): 366–74.

1556 "Report of the Special Committee on the Work of the Holy Spirit." A report of the Presbyterian Church of the U.S.A., Philadelphia, 1970.

1557 Reynolds, Terrence Paul. "The Coherence of Life Without God Before God: The Problem of Earthly Desires in the Later Theology of Dietrich Bonhoeffer." Unpublished dissertation, Brown University, 1983.

1558 Riaud, Alexis. *The Holy Spirit Acting in Our Souls.* Alba House, 1979.

1559 Rice, John R. *The Power of Pentecost.* Sword of the Lord Publishers, 1949.

1560 Richard, Jean. "Concu du Saint-Esprit, né de la Vierge Marie," *EgTh* 10 (October 1979): 291–321.

1561 Richard, Lucien. "The Enigma of Theologians in the Roman Catholic Church," *Enc* 42 (Autumn 1981): 329–51.

1562 Richards, Ellis H. "Kantian Ethics and the Pauline Doctrine of the Holy Spirit." Unpublished dissertation, Drew University, 1956.

1563 Richardson, R. *A Scriptural View of the Office of the Holy Spirit.* Chase & Hall, 1875.

1564 Richter, Gerhard. "Ansätze und Motive für die Lehre des Gregorios Palamas von den Göttlichen Energien," *OS* 31 (December 1982): 281–96.

1565 Ricketts, Ronald. *The Use of a Lectionary for Preaching Purposes in a Baptist Church.* Christian Theological Seminary, 1983.

1566 Riddell, John C. *The Calling of God.* Saint Andrews Press, 1961.

1567 Ridiger, Aleksiy, Metropolitan of Tallinn and Estonia. "Serving the World—in the Power of the Holy Spirit." 8th Conference of European Churches, October 18–25, 1979. 5 parts.

1568 Ridout, George W. *Spiritual Gifts, Including the Gift of Tongues: A Consideration of the Gifts of the Spirit and Particularly the Gift of Tongues, the "Pneumatika" and the "Charismata" of 1 Corinthians."* Nazarene Publishing House, n.d.

1569 Ridout, Samuel. *Person and Work of the Holy Spirit.* Loizeaux Brothers, n.d.

1570 Riedel, Warren C. "A Biblical Approach to the Gifts of the Holy Spirit." Unpublished master's thesis, Lancaster Theological Seminary, 1971.

1571 Riera, Camillo. *Doctrina de los Símbolos toledanos sobre el Espíritu Santo.* Balmesiana, 1955.

1572 Ries, Claude A. "The Holy Spirit and the Converted Man," in *Insights into Holiness,* Kenneth Geiger, editor. Beacon Hill Press, 1962. Pp. 191–200.

1573 Riggi, Calogero. "La Liturgia Della Pace Nella Prima Clementis," in *Fons Vivus: Eusebio Maria Vismara,* Armando Cuva, editor. Pas Verlag, 1971. Pp. 29–124.

1574 Riggs, Ralph M. *The Spirit Himself.* Gospel Publishing House, 1949.

1575 Riley, John E. "Holiness—Crisis and Process," in *Insights into Holiness,* Kenneth Geiger, editor. Beacon Hill Press, 1962. Pp. 91–106.

1576 Rimmer, Charles B. *The Unpredictable Wind: A Book on the Holy Spirit.* Nelson, 1974.

1577 Rippon, John. *Discourses on the All Sufficient Gracious Assistance of the Spirit of Christ.* J. Bateson, 1960.

1578 Ritchey, Mary G. "Khomiakov and His Theory of Sobornost," *Diak* 17:1 (1982): 53–62.

1579 Ritschl, Dietrich. "The History of the Filioque Controversy," in *Conflicts about the Holy Spirit,* Hans Küng and Jürgen Moltmann, editors. Seabury Press, 1979. Pp. 3–14.

1580 ______. "Warum wir Konzilien feiern Konstantinopel 381," *ThZ* 38 (July-August 1982): 213–25.

1581 Ritter, Adolf M. *Kerygma und Logos.* Vandenhoeck & Ruprecht, 1979.

1582 Roark, Warren C. *The Holy Spirit.* Warner Press, 1947.

1583 Robbins, Thomas. *A Discourse on the Doctrine of the Trinity.* S. Underwood, 1836.

1584 Robeck, Cecil M., Jr., ed. *Charismatic Experiences in History.* Hendrickson Publishers, 1986.

1585 ______. "Irenaeus and 'Prophetic Gifts,'" in *Essays on Apostolic Themes: Studies in Honor of Howard M. Ervin.* Paul Elbert, editor. Hendrickson Publishers, 1985. Pp. 104–14.

1586 Roberts, Frank C. "Gottfried Arnold on Historical Understanding: An Early Pietist Approach," *FH* 14:2 (Spring-Summer 1982): 50–59.

1587 Roberts, Harold. "The Holy Spirit and the Trinity," in *The Doctrine of the Holy Spirit,* Vincent Taylor, editor. Epworth, 1937. Pp. 105–28.

1588 Roberts, Norman L. "Paul's Conception of the Spirit of God in Relation to Man." Unpublished dissertation, Southern Baptist Seminary, 1949.

1589 Roberts, Oral. *The Baptism with the Holy Spirit and the Value of Speaking in Tongues Today.* Privately published, 1964.

1590 Roberts, Richard H. "Geist, Struktur und Wahrheit in der Kirche," in *Das Religiöse Bewusstsein und der Heilige Geist in der Kirche,* Klaus Kremkau, editor. Otto Lembeck, 1980. Pp. 11–42.

1591 Roberts, Richard M. *The Spirit of God and the Faith of Today.* Willet, Clark & Colby, 1930.

1592 Roberts, Robert C. "What is Spirituality," *RefJ* 33:8 (August 1983): 14–18.

1593 Robertson, John D. *The Holy Spirit and Christian Service.* Hodder & Stoughton, 1900.

1594 Robillard, Edmond. "Aux Sources de la Prière: L'Esprit-Saint dans l'Homme Nouveau," *ReSR* 50 (April 1976): 157–68.

1595 Robinson, Arthur W. *The Holy Spirit and the Individual.* SPCK, 1918.

1596 Robinson, Douglas. "The Ordo Salutis and Charismatic Movement," *Chm* 97:3 (1983): 232–43.

1597 Robinson, H. Wheeler. *The Christian Experience of the Holy Spirit.* James Nisbet & Company, 1928.

1598 Robinson, James M. *Das Problem des Heiligen Geistes bei Wilhelm Hermann.* Friedrichs Universitäts Buchruckerei, 1952.

1599 Robinson, Paul. *Call the Witnesses: Perspectives on Evangelism in the Church of the Brethren.* Brethren Press, 1974.

1600 Robson, John, of Ajmer. *The Holy Spirit: The Paraclete.* Funk & Wagnalls, 1895.

1601 Rodenberg, Otto. *Word und Geist.* R. Brockhaus, 1969.

1602 Roman Catholic World Methodist Council Joint Commission. "The Holy Spirit, Christian Experience, and Authority: Further Catholic/Methodist Reflections," *OC* 16:3 (1980): 225–33.

1603 Roman Catholic World Methodist Council Joint Commission. "The Holy Spirit: Papers Prepared for Roman Catholic-World Methodist Council Joint Commission," *OC* 16:3 (1980): 169–94.

1604 Romig, Mary Foster. "A Critical Edition of Peter Abelard's 'Exposition in Hexameron.' " Unpublished dissertation, University of Southern California, 1981.

1605 Rondet, H. "L'Esprit saint et l'Eglise, dans saint Augustin et dans l'augustinisme," in *L'Esprit Saint et L'Eglise.* Fayard, 1969. Pp. 153–78.

1606 Rosato, Philip J. "Called by God in the Holy Spirit: Pneumatological Insights into Ecumenism," *EcR* 30 (April 1978): 110–26.

1607 ______. *The Spirit as Lord: The Pneumatology of Karl Barth.* T. & T. Clark, 1981.

1608 ______. "Spirit Christology: Ambiguity and Promise," *ThSt* 38 (September 1977): 423–49.

1609 Rose, Delbert R. *A Theology of Christian Experience.* Bethany Fellowship, Inc., 1965.

1610 Ross, J. M. "How Did the Holy Spirit Get into the Trinity," *KTR* 5 (Autumn 1982): 59–80.

1611 Ross, Russ. "The Redemptive Model and the Holy Spirit's Work in Ethics," *BRR* 11:2 (1982): 28–42.

1612 Rossano, Piero. "La Parola e lo Spirito: Riflessioni su 1 Tess 1,5 E 1 Cor 2,4–5," in *Mélanges Bibliques,* Albert L. Descamps, editor. J. Duculot, 1970. Pp. 337–44.

1613 Rossum, Joost van. "Reflections on Byzantine Ecclesiology: Nicetas Stethatos' on the Hierarchy," *SVTQ* 25:2 (1981): 75–83.

1614 Rouse, William Thomas. *The Holy Spirit.* Sunday School Board of Southern Baptist Convention, 1935.

1615 Rowlands, Robert Tudor. "A Study for New Church Members Emphasizing the Doctrine of the United Church of Canada (Ontario)." Unpublished dissertation, Drew University, 1983.

1616 Rudvin, Arne. "Concept and Practice of Christian Mission," *IntRMiss* 65 (October 1976): 374–90.

1617 Ruler, A. A. van. "Structuurverschillen tussen het Christologische en het Pneumatologische gezichtspunt," in *De Spiritu Sancto.* Kemick, 1964. Pp. 205–22.

1618 Runyon, Theodore. "Testing the Spirits," in *What the Spirit Is Saying to the Churches,* Theodore Runyon, editor. Hawthorn Books, 1975. Pp. 105–21.

1619 ______, ed. *What the Spirit Is Saying to the Churches.* Hawthorn Books, 1975.

1620 Rusch, William G. "The Doctrine of the Holy Spirit in the Patristic and Medieval Church," in *The Holy Spirit in the Life of the Church: From Biblical Times to the Present,* Paul D. Opsahl, editor. Augsburg Publishing Co., 1978. Pp. 66–98.

1621 Rüsch, Theodor. *Die Entstehung der Lehre vom Heiligen Geist.* Zwingli Verlag, 1952.

1622 Russell, Norman. "Anselm of Havelberg and the Union of the Churches: Problem of the Filioque" (part 1), *Sob* NS 1:2 (1979): 19–41.

1623 ______. "Anselm of Havelberg and the Union of the Churches: Question of Authority" (part 2), *Sob* NS 2:1 (1980): 29–41.

1624 Rust, Eric Charles. "The Holy Spirit, Nature, and Man," *RE* 63:2 (Spring 1966): 157–76.

1625 ______. *The Old Testament Understanding of the Spirit of God.* N.p., n.d.

1626 Rylaarsdam, John C. "Hebrew Wisdom with Special Reference to the Concept of the Spirit." Unpublished dissertation, University of Chicago, 1945.

1627 Ryland, John Collett. *The Wonderful Extremes United in the Person of Christ.* M. Lewis, 1772.

1628 Ryle, Rodney K. "The Convicting Ministry of the Holy Spirit in John 16:8–11." Unpublished dissertation, Grace Theological Seminary, 1984.

1629 Ryrie, Charles C. *The Holy Spirit.* Moody Press, 1965.

S

1630 Saake, H. "Paulus als Ekstatiker: Pneumatologische Beobachtungen zu 2 Kor. 12:1–10," *Bib* 53:3 (1972): 404–10.

1631 Sabrey, Thomas W. "The Person and Work of the Holy Spirit in the Sanctification of Souls." Unpublished dissertation, Catholic University of America, 1953.

1632 Sadler, Gerald Allen. "Increasing the Sharing of the Pastoral Ministry with the Laity at Christian Life Church." Unpublished dissertation, Drew University, 1981.

1633 Sahagian, Samuel. "Temps de l'Eglise, Actes 2:1–13," *ETR* 58:3 (1983): 359–67.

1634 Sala, Harold J. "An Investigation of the Baptizing and Filling Work of the Holy Spirit in the New Testament Related to the Pentecostal Doctrine of 'Initial Evidence.' " Unpublished dissertation, Bob Jones University, 1966.

1635 Samarin, William J. "Glossolalia As a Vocal Phenomenon," in *Speaking in Tongues: Let's Talk About It,* Watson E. Mills, editor. Word Books, 1973. Pp. 128–42.

1636 Samartha, Stanley. "The Holy Spirit and People of Various Faiths, Cultures, and Ideologies," in *The Holy Spirit,* Dow Kirkpatrick, editor. Tidings, 1974. Pp. 20–39.

1637 ______. "Mission and Movements of Innovation," *M* 3 (April 1975): 143–54.

1638 Sambayya, E. "Blasphemy," *IJT* 2:1 (March 1953): 9–14.

1639 Samuel, Leith. *The Holy Spirit Today.* Pickering and Inglis, 1978.

1640 Sanders, J. Oswald. *The Holy Spirit and His Gifts.* Zondervan, 1970.

1641 ______. *The Holy Spirit of Promise.* Christian Literature Crusade, 1962.

1642 Sangster, W. E. *The Path of Perfection.* Abingdon-Cokesbury, 1943.

1643 Sauer, Walter K. "The Operation of the Holy Spirit as Revealed in the Book of Acts." Unpublished master's thesis, Western Evangelical Seminary, 1954.

1644 Sauter, Gerhard. "Geist und Freiheit: Geistvorstellungen und die Erwartung des Geistes," *EvTh* 41 (May-June 1981): 212–23.

1645 ______. "Zur Theologie des Heiligen Geistes," *EvTh* 41 (May-June 1981): 185–258.

1646 Saxer, Ernst. "Reformierte, Tauflehre in der Krise," *ThZ* 31 (March-April 1975): 95–107.

1647 Scaer, David P. "Formula of Concord Article VI: The Third Use of the Law," *CTQ* 42 (April 1978): 145–55.

1648 ______. "Problems of the Spirit, Pragmatically Speaking (Constantinople, 381 AD)," *CT* 25 (December 11, 1981): 12–13.

1649 Scanlan, Michael. "Power in Penance: Confession and the Holy Spirit," in *Spirit and the Church,* Ralph Martin, compiler. Pentecostal Publishing House, 1977. Pp. 315–18.

1650 Scerbo, Joseph Michael. "Reconciliation: The Purpose of Spirit-Directed Therapy." Unpublished dissertation, Graduate Theological Union, 1983.

1651 Schaberg, Jane. *The Father, the Son and the Holy Spirit: The Triadic Phrase in Matthew 28:19b.* Scholars Press, 1982.

1652 Schaeder, Erich A. *Das Geistproblem der Theologie.* A. Deichert, 1924.

1653 Schäfer, Peter. *Die Vorstellung vom Heiligen Geist in der rabbinischen Literatur.* Koesel Verlag, 1972.

1654 Schenk, Wolfgang. "Der Einfluss der Logienquelle auf das Markusevangelium," *ZNW* 70:3/4 (1979): 141–65.

1655 Schermann, Theodor. *Die gottheit des Heiligen Geistes.* Herder, 1901.

1656 Schick, Erich. *Psychologie und Heilige Geist.* Heinrich Maier, 1943.

1657 Schindler, Alfred. "Charis oder Charisma: Zur Entstehung einer bedenklichen Theologischen Alternative in der alten Kirche," *EvTh* 41 (May-June 1981): 235–43.

1658 Schlier, Heinrich. "Zum Begriff des Geistes nach dem Johannesevangelium," in *Neutestamentliche Aufsätze: Festschrfit für Prof. Josef Schmid zum 70. Geburtstag,* J. Blinzler, O. Kuss, and F. Pustet, 1963. Pp. 233–39.

1659 Schlink, Basilea, with John and Mary Foote and Michael Harper (trans.). *Ruled by the Spirit.* Lakeland, 1972.

1660 Schlitt, Dale M. "Holy Spirit Sent into the World," *EgTh* 6 (January 1975): 97–105.

1661 Schlorff, Samuel P. "Theological and Apologetical Dimensions of Muslim Evangelization," *WTJ* 42 (Spring 1980): 335–66.

1662 Schlütz, Karl. *Isaias 11,2 (die sieben Gaben des Hl. Geistes) in den ersten vier christlichen Jahrhunderten.* Aschendorff, 1932.

1663 Schmidt, Erik. "Hegel und die Kirchliche Trinitätslehre," *NZST* 24:3 (1982): 241–60.

1664 Schmidt, Karl Ludwig. *Die Pfingstergählung und das Pfingstereignis.* J. C. Hinrichs, 1919.

1665 ______. "Das Pneuma Hagion als Person und als Charisma," *EJ* 13 (1965): 187–231.

1666 Schmidt, Kenneth L. "Karl Barth's Theology of Prayer." Unpublished dissertation, Princeton Theological Seminary, 1980.

1667 Schmitt, Bruno. "Ein Eigenartiges Trinitäts und Verkündigungsbild: Ein Beiträg zur Ikonographie des Heiligen Geistes," in *In Verbo Tuo,* Alfons Altehenger, et al., editors. Stegler Verlag, 1963. Pp. 307–20.

1668 Schmitt, J. "Simples Remarques sur le Fragment Jn 20:22–23," *RSciRel* 4 (1956): 415–23.

1669 Schnackenburg, Rudolf. "Die Johanneische Gemeinde und ihre Gesiterfahrung," in *Die Kirche des Anfanges,* Rudolf Schnackenburg, editor. 1977. Pp. 277–30.

1670 Schneider, Herbert. "Baptism in the Holy Spirit in the New Testament," in *The Holy Spirit and Power,* K. McDonnel, editor. Catholic Charismatic Renewal, 1975. Pp. 35–55.

1671 Schnepel, Erich. "Der biblische Weg zu Vermehrter Geistesausrüstung," in *Freude im Dienst: Arno Haun,* Hans Bruns, editor. Verlag der Francke-Buchhandlung, 1961. Pp. 98–103.

1672 Schoeman, P. C. "Word and Spirit: Relevance of Scripture for a Doctrine of the Holy Spirit," in *The Spirit in Biblical Perspective,* W. S. Vorster, editor. University of South Africa, 1980. Pp. 19–38.

1673 Schoenborn, Christoph von, et al. *Die charismatische Erneuerung und die Kirchen.* Pustet, 1977.

1674 Schonebaum, William J. "The Holy Spirit in the Life of the Believing Community." Unpublished dissertation, Luther-Northwestern Seminaries, 1979.

1675 Schoonenberg, Piet. "Het doopsel met Heilige Geest," in *Leven uit de geest*. Hilversum, 1974. Pp.165 – 86.

1676 ______. "Notities over Charismata," in *Charismatisch Nederland,* F. Rutke, editor. N.p. 1977. Pp. 43 – 61.

1677 ______. with H. Hoskins (trans.). "Baptism with the Holy Spirit," in *Experience of the Spirit,* edited by Peter Huizing and William Bassett. Seabury Press, 1974. Pp. 20 – 37.

1678 Schreiner, Thomas Robert. "Circumcision: An Entree into 'Newness' in Pauline Thought." Unpublished dissertation, Fuller Theological Seminary, 1983.

1679 Schützeichel, Heribert. "Calvins Kritik an der Firmung," in *Zeichen des Glaubens.* Benziger Verlag, 1972. Pp. 123 – 35.

1680 Schultze, Bernhard. "Zum Ursprung des Filioque: Das Filioque und der Römische Primat," *OCP* 48:1 (1982): 5 – 18.

1681 Schwarz, Hans. "Reflections on the Work of the Spirit Outside the Church," *NZST* 23:3 (1981): 197 – 211.

1682 Schwarzwäller, Klaus. "Zur Struktur von Luthers Pneumatologie," in *Lutherjahrbuch 1971,* Franz Lau, editor. Friedrich Wittig Verlag, 1971. Pp. 26 – 58.

1683 Schweizer, Eduard. "Esprit et communauté chez Paul et ses disciples," in *L'Esprit Saint et L'Eglise.* Fayard, 1969. Pp. 45 – 70.

1684 ______. "πνεῦμα, πνευματικός" in *Theological Dictionary of the New Testament,* Gerhard Kittel, editor. 10 vols. Eerdmans Publishing Co., 1964. 6:332 – 451.

1685 ______. "Was ist der Heilige Geist? Eine bibel-theologische Hindführung," *Concil* 15:10 (1979): 494 – 98.

1686 ______. "What is the Holy Spirit? A Study in Biblical Theology," in *Conflicts about the Holy Spirit,* Hans Küng and Jürgen Moltmann, editors. Seabury Press, 1979. Pp. ix – xvi.

1687 Schweizer, Eduard, with A. E. Harvey (trans.). *The Spirit of God.* Adam and Charles Black, 1960.

1688 Schweizer, Eduard, with Reginald H. and Ilse Fuller (trans.). *The Holy Spirit.* Fortress Press, 1980.

1689 Scofield, Cyrus Ingerson. *Plain Papers on the Doctrine of the Holy Spirit.* Baker Book House, 1966.

1690 Scott, C. Anderson. *The Fellowship of the Spirit.* J. Clark, 1921.

1691 Scott, Ernest F. *I Believe in the Holy Spirit.* Abingdon Press, 1958.

1692 ______. *The Spirit in the New Testament.* Doran, 1923.

1693 Scouteris, Constantine. "Paradosis: The Orthodox Understanding of Tradition," *Sob* NS 4:1 (1982): 30–37.

1694 Scraper, Randy Lee. "The Baptism with the Holy Spirit." Unpublished master's thesis, Oral Roberts University, 1979.

1695 Scribner, William. *Pray for the Holy Spirit.* Anson D. F. Randolph, 1875.

1696 Scroggie, W. Graham. *The Baptism of the Holy Spirit and Speaking with Tongues.* Marshall, Morgan & Scott, 1956.

1697 ______. *Speaking in Tongues.* Book Stall, 1919.

1698 Scroggs, Robin. "The Exaltation of the Spirit by Some Early Christians," *JBL* 84 (1965): 359–73.

1699 Seabury, Samuel. *Discourses Illustrative of the Nature and Work of the Holy Spirit.* Pott, Young & Co., 1874.

1700 Sears, Robert Thomas. "Spirit—Divine and Human: The Theology of the Holy Spirit of Heribert Muehlen and Its Relevance for Evaluating the Data of Psychotherapy." Unpublished dissertation, Fordham University, 1974.

1701 Sebree, Herbert T. "Glossolalia," in *The Word and the Doctrine,* Kenneth E. Geiger, editor. Beacon Hill Press, 1965. Pp. 335–52.

1702 Selby, Thomas G. *The Holy Spirit and Christian Privilege.* Charles H. Kelly, 1894.

1703 Sell, Alan P. F. "Transcendence, Immanence and the Supernatural," *JTSA* 26 (March 1979): 56–66.

1704 Sellin, Gerhard. "Das 'Geheimnis' der Weisheit und das Rätsel der 'Christuspartei' (zu 1 Kor 1–4)," *ZNW* 73:1 (1982): 69–96.

1705 Semaan, Wanis A. "The Holy Spirit and the Ecumenical Movement," *RefW* 37:8 (December 1983): 278–82.

1706 Sesboue, Bernard. "Bulletin de Théologie dogmatique: Trinité et Pneumatologie," *ReSR* 66 (July-September 1978): 417–60.

1707 Seyer, Herman D. *The Stewardship of Spiritual Gifts: A Study of First Corinthians.* Fleetwood Art Studios, 1974.

1708 Shapland, C. R. B. *The Letters of St. Athanasius Concerning the Holy Spirit.* Epworth, 1951.

1709 Sharpe, Eric J. "Spirit and the Religions," in *The Church Crossing Frontiers: B. Sundkler,* Peter Beyerhaus, editor. Gleerup, 1969. Pp. 111–23.

1710 Shaub, Robert William. "An Analysis of the Healing Ministries Conducted in Three Contemporary Churches." Unpublished dissertation, Eastern Baptist Seminary, 1980.

1711 Shaw, John Mackintosh. *The Belief in the Holy Spirit.* Stirling, 1936.

1712 Shaw, Mark Randolph. "The Marrow of Practical Divinity: A Study in the Theology of William Perkins." Unpublished dissertation, Westminster Theological Seminary, 1981.

1713 Shelter, Sanford G. "The Holy Spirit and Church Administration," in *Encounter with the Holy Spirit,* George R. Brunk, II, editor. Herald Press, 1972. Pp. 156–73.

1714 Shepard, Darrell Royce. "The Sensibility of 'Holy Spirit.' " Unpublished dissertation, University of Nebraska/Lincoln, 1968.

1715 Shepherd, Richard Lawson. "The Awakening of 1904–1908 and Its Effects on Baptists in the United States." Unpublished dissertation, Southwestern Baptist Seminary, 1982.

1716 Sherry, Patrick. "Are Spirits Bodiless Persons?" *NZST* 24:1 (1982): 37–52.

1717 ______. "A Neglected Argument for Immortality (Indwelling of the Holy Spirit)," *RelSt* 19 (March 1983): 13–24.

1718 ______. *Spirit, Saints, and Immortality.* University of New York Press, 1984.

1719 Shimizu, Mitsuo. "Epistemology in the Thought of John Wesley." Unpublished dissertation, Drew University, 1980.

1720 Shirley, Walter Augustus. *The Supremacy of Holy Scripture.* J. Vincent, 1847.

1721 Shoemaker, Samuel M. *With the Holy Spirit and with Fire.* Harper and Row, 1960.

1722 Shoemaker, W. R. "The Use of *Ruach* in the Old Testament and of *Pneuma* in the New Testament," *JBL* 23 (1904): 13–67.

1723 Short, Augustus. *The Witness of the Spirit with Our Spirit.* J. Parker & Company, 1846.

1724 Shuler, John Lewis. *By Water and By Fire: The Work of the Holy Spirit in the Life*. Review and Herald Publishing Association, 1976.

1725 Siman, Amanouil P. "Die pneumatische Dimension der Eucharistie nach der Überlieferung der Syrischen Kirche," in *Oriens Christianus, BD 60,* J. Molitor, editor. Patmos Verlag, 1976. Pp. 100–121.

1726 Siman, Emmanuel P. "Dimension Pneumatique de l'Eucharistie d'après la tradition Syrienne D'Antioche," in *L'Expérience de l'Esprit,* P. Brand, et al., editors. N.p., 1976. Pp. 303–31.

1727 ______. *L'Expérience de l'Esprit par l'Eglise*. Beauchesne, 1971.

1728 ______. De pnematologische dimensie van de eucharistic volgens de Syrische traditie van Antiochië," in *Leven uit de geest*. Hilversum, 1974. Pp. 87–104.

1729 Simmers, Marvin, ed. *Church Studies on the Holy Spirit* John Knox Press, 1983.

1730 Simon, John S. *John Wesley and the Methodist Societies*. Epworth, 1923.

1731 Simons, John David. "ΠΑΡΑΚΛΗΤΟΣ in the Johannine Writings." Unpublished dissertation, Southern Baptist Seminary, 1928.

1732 Simpson, A. B. *Emblems of the Holy Spirit*. Christian Alliance Publishing Company, 1901.

1733 ______. *The Holy Spirit, or Power from on High*. Christian Alliance Publishing Company, 1924.

1734 Sinclair, Clarence H. "The Church as the Communion of the Holy Spirit: A Study of the Relationship Between the Doctrine of the Holy Spirit and the Doctrine of the Church." Unpublished master's thesis, Princeton Theological Seminary, 1952.

1735 Sirks, G. J. "The Cinderella of Theology: The Doctrine of the Holy Spirit," *HTR* 50 (April 1957): 77–89.

1736 Sisk, Ronald Douglas. "The Ethics of Henlee Barnette: A Study in Method." Unpublished dissertation, Southern Baptist Seminary, 1982.

1737 Sklba, Richard J. " 'Until the Spirit From on High is Poured Out on Us' (Isa 32:15): Reflections on the Role of the Spirit in Exile," *CBQ* 46 (January 1984): 1–17.

1738 Slattery, Charles L. *The Light Within: A Study of the Holy Spirit*. Longmans, Green & Co., 1915.

1739 Slevin, Bernard. *Little Office of the Holy Ghost.* Paraclete Press, 1958.

1740 Slosser, Bob. *See How the Wind Blows: The Holy Spirit Nudges the Church Toward Unity.* Logos International, 1980.

1741 Slover, James David. "Representative Current Approaches to the Doctrine of the Holy Spirit." Unpublished dissertation, Southwestern Baptist Seminary, 1970.

1742 Sluys, J. C. M. van der. "Om Het Geloof en Zijn Vastheid," in *In Open Veld: G. J. Sirks,* Johan Brinkmann, et al., editors. N.p. 1962. Pp. 122–37.

1743 Smail, Thomas Allen. *Reflected Glory: The Spirit in Christ and Christians.* Eerdmans Publishing Co., 1975.

1744 Smalley, Stephen S. "Spiritual Gifts and 1 Corinthians 12–16," *JBL* 88 (1968): 427–33.

1745 Smeaton, George. *The Doctrine of the Holy Spirit.* T. & T. Clark, 1889.

1746 Smeeton, Donald D. "A Pentecostal Looks Again at Vatican II," *P* 5:1 (Spring 1983): 34–45.

1747 ______. "The Pneumatology of William Tyndale," *P* 3:1 (Spring 1981): 22–30.

1748 Smith, Aaron A. *The Holy Spirit and His Workings.* Privately published, n.d.

1749 Smith, Charles Edward. *The Baptism of Fire.* D. Lothrup and Company, 1883.

1750 Smith, D. Moody. "John 16:1–15," *Int* 33 (January 1979): 58–62.

1751 Smith, David. *The Testimony of the Holy Spirit.* The Christian Irishman, n.d.

1752 Smith, Elbert Newell. "Developing 'Koinonia' as a Cohesive Element Within the Administrative Committee of a Local Congregation." Unpublished dissertation, Eastern Baptist Seminary, 1980.

1753 Smith, John P. *On the Personality and Divinity of the Holy Spirit.* Holdsworth and Ball, 1831.

1754 Smith, Jonathan Ritchie. *The Holy Spirit in the Gospels.* Macmillan, 1926.

1755 Smith, Joseph H. *Things of the Spirit.* Chicago Evangelistic Institute, 1940.

1756 Smith, Kenneth G. "The 'Mystery' of the Holy Spirit," *BBFL* 19 (January-March 1964): 3–6.

1757 Smith, Miles W. *On Whom the Spirit Came.* Judson Press, 1948.

1758 Smith, Robert E. "The Work of the Holy Spirit in the Upbuilding of the Church." Unpublished thesis, Princeton Theological Seminary, 1943.

1759 Smith, Timothy L. *Called Unto Holiness.* Nazarene Publishing House, 1962.

1760 ______. "The Holy Spirit in the Hymns of the Wesleys," *WTJ* 16 (Fall 1981): 20–47.

1761 ______. *Revivalism and Social Reform.* Abingdon Press, 1957.

1762 Smolik, Josef. "Filioque in the Reformed Tradition," *CV* 24:2 (1981): 219–22.

1763 Smylie, James H. "Reconciliation and Liberation: The Confession of 1967 (Symposium Papers, Princeton Theological Seminary, October 21–22, 1982)," *JPH* 61 (Spring 1983): 1–196.

1764 ______. "Testing the Spirits in the American Context: Great Awakenings, Pentecostalism, and the Charismatic Movements," *Int* 33 (1979): 32–46.

1765 Smythe, H. R. "Interpretation of Amos 4:13 in St. Athanasius and Didymus," *JTS* ns 1 (October 1950): 158–68.

1766 Snaith, Norman H. "The Meaning of 'The Paraclete,'" *ExT* 57 (1945–1946): 47–50.

1767 ______. "The Spirit of God in Jewish Thought," in *The Doctrine of the Holy Spirit,* Vincent Taylor, editor. Epworth, 1937. Pp. 9–37.

1768 Snyder, Howard A. "The Church as Holy Charismatic," *WTJ* 15 (Fall 1980): 7–32.

1769 Söhngen, Gottlieb. "Der Geist der Einsicht und der Liebe, eine Ansprache," *Cat* 23 (1969): 294–97.

1770 Soltau, George. *Person and Mission of the Holy Spirit.* Philadelphia School of the Bible, n.d.

1771 Song, Yong Jo. "The Holy Spirit and Mission: Toward a Biblical Understanding of the Holy Spirit in Relation to the Mission of the Church with Special Reference to Contemporary Religious Movements in Korea." Unpublished dissertation, Fuller Theological Seminary, 1981.

1772 Soper, David W. *The Spirit is Willing.* Westminster Press, 1958.

1773 Sopko, Andrew J. "'Palamism before Palamas' and the Theology of Gregory of Cyprus," *SVTQ* 23:3–4 (1979): 139–47.

1774 Soren, Anthony M. *How to Receive the Holy Spirit.* Revell Co., 1971.

1775 Southey, Robert. *The Life of John Wesley and the Rise and Progress of Methodism.* Longman, Brown, and Green, 1846.

1776 Spidlik, Tomas. "L'Icone, Manifestation du Monde Spirituel," *Greg* 61:3 (1980): 539–54.

1777 Spoerlein, Bernhard. "Das Charisma im Neuen Testament," in *Mystik,* A. Resch, editor. N.p., 1975. Pp. 112–34.

1778 Spurgeon, Charles Haddon. *Twelve Sermons on the Holy Spirit.* Revell Co., n.d.

1779 Staats, Reinhart. "Die Basilianische Verherrlichung des Heiligen Geistes auf dem Konzil zu Konstantinopel 381: 'Kerygma und Dogma,' " *KD* 25 (October-December 1979): 232–53.

1780 Stacey, John, et al., eds. *Doing Theology: An Introduction for Preachers.* Local Preachers' Department of the Methodist Church, 1972.

1781 Stafford, Thomas P. *A Study of the Holy Spirit.* Judson Press, 1920.

1782 Stagg, Frank. *The Holy Spirit Today.* Broadman Press, 1973.

1783 Stagg, Frank and James Buchanan Harrison. "The Holy Spirit in the New Testament," *RE* 63:2 (Spring 1966): 135–48.

1784 Stählin, Wilhelm. *Die Bitte um den Heiligen Geist.* Evangelisches Verlag, 1969.

1785 Stalder, Kurt. *Das Werk des Geistes in der Heiligung bei Paulus.* EVZ Verlag, 1962.

1786 Stamps, Drure Fletcher. "The Authority of the Holy Spirit." Unpublished dissertation, Southern Baptist Seminary, 1920.

1787 Stanger, Frank B. "The Church and the Spirit," in *Further Insights into Holiness,* Kenneth Geiger, editor. Beacon Hill Press, 1963. Pp. 213–30.

1788 Staniloae, Dumitru. "The Procession of the Holy Spirit from the Father and His Relation to the Son, as the Basis of our Deification and Adoption," in *Spirit of God, Spirit of Christ,* L. Vischer, editor. World Council of Churches, 1981. N.p.

1789 Starkey, Lycurgus. "The Holy Spirit and the Wesleyan Witness," *RL* 49 (Spring 1980): 72–80.

1790 ______. *The Holy Spirit at Work in the Church.* Abingdon Press, 1964.

1791 ______. *The Work of the Holy Spirit.* Abingdon Press, 1962.

1792 ______. "The Work of the Holy Spirit in the Theology of John Wesley." Unpublished dissertation, Columbia University, 1953.

1793 Steele, Daniel. *The Gospel of the Comforter.* Christian Witness Company, 1897.

1794 Stegmann, Basil. "Pentecost," *Wor* 26:7 (1952): 337–41.

1795 Steiger, Renate. "Die Lebendigkeit des Erkennenden Geistes bei Nikolaus von Kues," in *Das Menschenbild des Nikolaus von Kues,* Martin Bodweig, et al., editors. Matthias-Grünewald-Verlag, 1978. N.p.

1796 Stephanou, Eusebius A. "Charismata in the Early Church Fathers," *GOTR* 21 (Summer 1976): 125–46.

1797 Stephens, Elizabeth C. "Goodbye, My Pentecost," *SLJ* 21 (December 1977): 49–59.

1798 Stephens, Peter. "The Gifts of the Spirit in the Church," in *The Holy Spirit,* Dow Kirkpatrick, editor. Tidings, 1974. Pp. 125–57.

1799 ______. *The Holy Spirit in the Theology of Martin Buber.* Cambridge University Press, 1970.

1800 Stettinger, Gottfried. *Der Paraklet: Detailstudie aus den johanneischen Abscheidsreden.* Verlag Mayer and Kamp, 1922.

1801 Steuer, Axel D. and James W. McClendon. *Is God God?* Abingdon Press, 1981.

1802 Stevens, David Mark. "John Cotton and Thomas Hooker: The Rhetoric of the Holy Spirit." Unpublished dissertation, University of California/Berkeley, 1972.

1803 Stewart, George. *God in Our Street.* Abingdon Press, 1939.

1804 Stibbs, Alan Marshall. *The Spirit Within You.* Baker Book House, 1979.

1805 Stichart, Franz O. *Die Lehre vom Beustande des Heiligen Geistes.* Johann F. Hartknock, 1835.

1806 Stiles, John E. *The Gift of the Holy Spirit.* Privately published, n.d.

1807 ______. *How to Receive the Holy Spirit.* Revell Co., 1971.

1808 Stine, Esther C. "The Cry from the Outside: The Communion of the Holy Spirit," *JPH* 61 (Spring 1983): 55–65.

1809 Stinnett, Charles R. "On the Nature of Gifts and Gift-Giving," *JPC* 8 (Winter 1954): 218–22.

1810 Stoffer, Dale Rupert. "The Background and Development of Thought and Practice in the German Baptist Brethren (Dunker) and the Brethren (Progressive) Churches (c. 1650–1979)." Unpublished dissertation, Fuller Theological Seminary, 1980.

1811 Stokes, Mark Boyd. *The Holy Spirit and Christian Experience.* Graded Press, 1975.

1812 Stollberg, Dietrich. "Heiliger Geist und Spiritualität in der deutschsprachigen Praktischen Theologie der Gegenwart," in *Das religiöse Bewusstsein und der Heilige Geist in der Kirche,* Klaus Kremkau, editor. Otto Lembeck, 1980. Pp. 45–52.

1813 Stonehouse, N. B. "Repentance, Baptism, and the Gift of the Holy Spirit," *WTJ* 13 (November 1950): 1–18.

1814 Stosch, Georg. *Die Wirksamkeit des Heiligen Geistes in der apostolischen zeit und in der Gegenwart.* C. Bertelsmann, 1900.

1815 Stott, John R. W. *Baptism and Fulness: The Work of the Holy Spirit.* InterVarsity Press, 1976.

1816 Stover, Dale Arden. "The Pneumatology of John Owen: A Study of the Role of the Holy Spirit in Relation to the Shape of a Theology." Unpublished dissertation, McGill University (Canada), 1967.

1817 Stover, Gene. *He Shall Baptize You with the Holy Ghost.* Privately published, n.d.

1818 Stowell, William Hendry. *On the Work of the Spirit.* Jackson and Wolford, 1849.

1819 Strachan, Gordon. "Theological and Cultural Origins of the Nineteenth Century Pentecostal Movement," in *Essays on Apostolic Themes: Studies in Honor of Howard M. Ervin.* Paul Elbert, editor. Hendrickson Publishers, 1985. Pp. 144–57.

1820 Strafford, Thomas Polhill. *A Study of the Holy Spirit.* Judson Press, 1920.

1821 Straton, Hillyer H. "The Divine Spirit and the Human Spirit in the Christian Life," *Found* 1:1 (1958): 65–72.

1822 Strauss, Lehman. *The Third Person: Seven Devotional Studies on the Person and Work of the Holy Spirit.* Loizeaux Brothers, 1954.

1823 Streeter, Burnett H. *The Spirit: The Relation of God and Man.* Macmillan, 1919.

1824 Strong, Edmund Linwood. *The Revelation of the Holy Spirit.* N.p., 1934.

1825 Strong, Stanley R. "Christian Counseling with Homosexuals," *JPTh* 8 (Winter 1980): 279–87.

1826 Stronstad, Roger. *The Charismatic Theology of St. Luke.* Hendrickson Publishers, 1986.

1827 ______. "The Influence of the Old Testament on the Charismatic Theology of St. Luke," *P* 2:1 (Spring 1980): 32–50.

1828 Stroumsa, Gedaliahu G. "Aspects de l'eschatologie Manicheenne," *RHR* 198 (April-June 1981): 163–81.

1829 ______. "Le couple de l'ange et de l'esprit: Traditions juives et Chrétiennes," *RBib* 88 (January 1981): 42–61.

1830 Stuckenbruck, Earl R. "The Spirit at Pentecost," in *Essays on New Testament Christianity,* C. R. Wetzel, editor. Evangel Publishing House, 1978. Pp. 34–51.

1831 Studer, Gerald C. "The Energizing Work of the Holy Spirit," in *Encounter with the Holy Spirit,* George R. Brunk, II, editor. Herald Press, 1972. Pp. 114–35.

1832 Stylianopoulos, Theodore. "A Christological Reflection," in *Jesus Christ: The Life of the World,* Ion Bria, editor. World Council of Churches, 1982. N.p.

1833 Sublon, Roland. "Esprit-Saint, Loi et Plaisir," *ReSR* 70 (January-March 1982): 151–60.

1834 Suenens, Léon Josef. "Come, Holy Spirit," in *Spirit and the Church,* Ralph Martin, compiler. Pentecostal Publishing House, 1977. Pp. 3–16.

1835 ______. "Holy Spirit: Our Hope," *Wor* 49 (May 1975): 254–62.

1836 Suenens, Léon J., with Francis Martin (trans.). *A New Pentecost?* Seabury Press, 1974.

1837 Suh, Yung-Ho. "The Spirit of Christ and Christian Living: A Study of Caspar Schwenckfeld's Christological Pneumatology." Unpublished dissertation, Temple University, 1982.

1838 Sullivan, Francis A. " 'Baptism in the Holy Spirit': A Catholic Interpretation of the Pentecostal Experience," *Greg* 55 (1974): 49–66.

1839 ______. " 'Speaking in Tongues' in the New Testament and in Modern Charismatic Renewal," in *The Spirit of God in Christian Life,* Edward Malatesta, editor. Paulist Press, 1977. Pp. 23–74.

1840 Sundara Rao, Rayi Ratna. "The Bhakti Element in Andhra Kraistava Kirtanalu: An Intensive Study of the Phenomenon of 'Bhakti,' A Sanskrit Word for Devotion, as Presented in the 'Telugu Christian Hymnal.'" Unpublished dissertation, University of Wisconsin/Madison, 1981.

1841 Swanson, Edwin C. "The Holy Spirit in His Redemptive Work." Unpublished thesis, Western Conservative Baptist Seminary, 1939.

1842 Sweet, Leonard I. *New Life in the Spirit.* Westminster Press, 1982.

1843 Swete, Henry Barclay. "Holy Spirit," in *A Dictionary of the Bible,* James Hastings, editor. 5 vols. Scribner's, 1902. 2:402–11.

1844 ______. *The Holy Spirit in the Ancient Church.* Macmillan, 1912.

1845 ______. *The Holy Spirit in the New Testament: A Study of Primitive Christian Teaching.* Macmillan, 1910.

1846 ______. *On the History of the Doctrine of the Procession of the Holy Spirit from the Apostolic Age to the Death of Charlemagne.* George Bell and Sons, 1876.

1847 Swiderski, Stanislaw. "Notion of the Trinity and Triadic Thought in the Fang People of Gabon," *RCEA* 9:2 (1975).

1848 Sykes, S. W. and J. P. Clayton. *Christ, Faith and History: Cambridge Studies in Christology.* Cambridge University Press, 1972.

1849 Synan, H. Vinson, ed. *Aspects of Pentecostal-Charismatic Origins.* Logos International, 1975.

T

1850 Taber, Charles R. "Limits of Indigenization in Theology," *M* 6 (January 1978): 53–79.

1851 Tappeiner, Daniel A. "Psychological Paradigm for the Interpretation of the Charismatic Phenomenon of Prophecy," *JPTh* 5 (Winter 1977): 23–29.

1852 ______. "Sacramental Causality in Aquinas and Rahner: Some Critical Thoughts," *SJT* 28:3 (1975): 243–57.

1853 Taylor, J. Z. "The Witness of the Holy Spirit," in *A Symposium on the Holy Spirit.* John Burns, 1879. Pp. 102–15.

1854 Taylor, John Vernon. *The Go-Between God.* SCM Press, 1972.

1855 Taylor, Rilla Dee. "The Conceptual Model for the Professional Practice of Seventh-Day Adventist Educational Administration Based on Proclamations of the Three Angels of Revelation 14." Unpublished dissertation, Andrews University, 1980.

1856 Taylor, Vincent. "The Spirit in the New Testament," in *The Doctrine of the Holy Spirit,* Vincent Taylor, editor. Epworth, 1937. Pp. 39–68.

1857 Taylor, Willard H. "Baptism with the Holy Spirit: Promise of Grace or Judgment?" *WTJ* 12 (Spring 1977): 16–25.

1858 Telford, John, ed. *The Letters of the Rev. John Wesley.* 8 vols. Epworth, 1931.

1859 Tenney, Merrill C. "Topics from the Gospel of John," (4 parts) *BS* 132 (January-December 1975).

1860 Terry, Bruce. "Baptized in One Spirit," *RQ* 21:4 (1978): 193–200.

1861 Thielicke, Helmut, with Geoffrey W. Bromiley (trans.). *The Evangelical Faith, V 3: The Holy Spirit, the Church, and Eschatology.* Eerdmans Publishing Co., 1981.

1862 Thiering, Barbara E. "Qumran Initiation and New Testament Baptism," *NTS* 27 (October 1981): 615–31.

1863 Thiessen, Henry Clarence. "The Holy Spirit in the Epistle to the Romans." Unpublished dissertation, Southern Baptist Seminary, 1929.

1864 Tholin, Richard. "The Holy Spirit and Liberation Movements: The Response of the Church," in *The Holy Spirit,* Dow Kirkpatrick, editor. Tidings, 1974. Pp. 40–75.

1865 Thomas, George F. *Spirit and Its Freedom.* University of North Carolina Press, 1939.

1866 Thomas, Robert L. "Now Concerning Spiritual Gifts: A Study of 1 Corinthians 12–14." Unpublished notebook, 1974.

1867 ______. "Tongues Will Cease," *JETS* 17:2 (1978): 81–89.

1868 Thomas, W. H. Griffith. *The Holy Spirit of God.* The Bible Institute Colportage Association, 1913.

1869 Thompson, Joseph P. *The Holy Comforter: His Person and His Work.* A. D. F. Randolph, 1866.

1870 Thom, Robert. *The Holy Spirit and the Name.* N.p., n.d.

1871 Thomson, James G. S. S. "Spiritual Gifts," in *Baker's Dictionary of Theology,* Everett Harrison, editor. Baker Book House, 1960. Pp. 497–504.

1872 Thomson, W. S. "Tongues at Pentecost: Acts 2," *ExT* 38 (1926–27): 284–86.

1873 Thrall, Margaret E. "Christian Vocation Today," *TH* 79 (March 1976): 84–89.

1874 Tice, Terrance Nelson. *Come, Creator Spirit.* Alliance of Reformed Churches, 1963.

1875 Tidings, Judy. *Gathering a People: Catholic Saints in Charismatic Perspective.* Logos International, 1977.

1876 Tiede, David L. "Acts 2:1–47," *Int* 33 (January 1979): 62–67.

1877 ______. "It Seemed Good to Us and the Holy Spirit: Comments on Lutheran-United Methodist Statement on Baptism," *QR* 1 (Fall 1980): 75–79.

1878 Tilak, S. John. "Nature, History and Spirit: A Theological Investigation on Nature, History and Spirit in Trialogue Among Western Secularism, Hindu Spiritualism and Christian Trinitarian Faith." Unpublished dissertation, Lutheran School of Theology at Chicago, 1977.

1879 ______. "The Office and Work of the Holy Spirit by Luther in the Light of the Idea of Spirit as Interpreted by Radhakrishnan and Aurobindo," *RS* 27 (September 1980): 72–84.

1880 Tillard, Jean M. R. "Eglise Catholique et Dialogues Bilateraux," *Iren* 56:1 (1983): 5–19.

1881 ______. "L'Eglise de Dieu est une Communion," *Iren* 53:4 (1980): 451–68.

1882 ______. "Jesus Christ, The Life of the World," *MSt* 21 (October 1982): 460–72.

1883 Timiadis, Emilianos. "The Centrality of the Holy Spirit in Orthodox Worship," *EP* 60 (1978): 317–57.

1884 ______. "Holy Spirit and the Mystical in Orthodox Theology," *LW* 23:3 (1976): 175–79.

1885 ______. "Life Giving: An Interpersonal Action," *Diak* 17:2 (1982): 109–26.

1886 Tinder, Donald G. "The Holy Spirit from Pentecost to the Present: Book Survey," *CT* 19 (May 19, 1975): 11–12.

1887 Tippett, Alan R. *God, Man and Church Growth: A Festschrift in Honor of Donald Anderson McGavran.* Eerdmans Publishing Co., 1973.

1888 Tomsky, Alexander. "John Paul II in Poland: Pilgrim of the Holy Spirit," *ComL* 7 (Autumn 1979): 160–65.

1889 Toon, Vita. "Charismatic Experience and Church Membership," *Chm* 90 (July-September 1976): 206–16.

1890 Torrance, Thomas F. "Une Contribution aux Recherches de Foi et Constitution sur le Ministère Ordone," *Istina* 19 (October-December 1974): 427–34.

1891 ______. "The Epistemological Relevance of the Holy Spirit," in *God and Rationality.* Oxford University Press, 1971. Pp. 164–92.

1892 ______. "La mission de l'Eglise," in *L'Esprit Saint et L'Eglise.* Fayard, 1969. Pp. 275–94.

1893 ______. "La Portée de la Doctrine du Saint-Esprit pour la théologiea Oecumenique," in *Hommage à Edmund Schlink,* Nikos A. Nissiotis, et al., editors. Verbum Caro, 1963. Pp. 166–76.

1894 Torrey, Reuben A. *The Baptism with the Holy Spirit.* Revell Co., 1897.

1895 ______. *The Holy Spirit: Who He Is and What He Does.* Revell Co., 1927.

1896 ______. *The Person and Work of the Holy Spirit.* Revell Co., 1910.

1897 Tosetti, Wilhelm. *Die Person des Heiligen Geistes in den Evangelien.* Hauptmann, 1910.

1898 Toynbee, Philip. *Towards the Holy Spirit.* SCM Press, 1982.

1899 Tozer, A. W. *How to be Filled with the Holy Spirit.* Christian Publications, Inc., n.d.

1900 Trape, Agostino. "Nota Sulla Processione Dello Spirito Santo Nella Teologia Trinitaria di S. Agostino e di S. Tommaso," in *San Tommaso,* Carlo Giacon, et al., editors. Città Nuova Editrice, 1975. Pp. 119–25.

1901 Treurnicht, Andries P. *Die Heilige Gees: Dir Geheim van Pinksterlewe.* Stellenbosch, 1960.

1902 Triacca, Achille M. "Spirito Santo e Liturgia: Linee Metodologiche per un Approfondimento," in *Lex Orandi, Lex Credendi,* Gerardo J. Békés and Giustino Farnedi, editors. Editrice Anselmiana, 1980. Pp. 132–64.

1903 Triebel, Johannes. "Strukturen des Bekennens: Beobachtungen zur Confessio Augustana und unserem Bekennen," *KD* 28 (October-December 1980): 317–26.

1904 Trocmé, E. "Le Saint-Esprit et l'Eglise, d'après le livre des Actes," in *L'Esprit Saint et L'Eglise.* Fayard, 1969. Pp. 19–27.

1905 Tsanana, Georgiou A. "Ta en te ekklesia charismata tou agiou pneumatos kata ton basileiou," in *Theologikon Symposion: P. K. Chretou,* Georg I. Mantzarides, et al., editors. N.p., 1967. Pp. 121–40.

1906 Tschude, Stephan. "Pinsepreken," *NTTid* 77:2 (1976): 65–74.

1907 Tugwell, Simon. *Did you Receive the Spirit?* Darton, Longman, and Todd, 1972.

1908 ______. "Reflections on the Pentecostal Doctrine of 'Baptism in the Holy Spirit,' " *HJ* 13 (1972): 260–81; 402–14.

1909 Tugwell, Simon, George Every, John O. Mills, and Peter Hocken, eds. *New Heaven, New Earth: An Encounter with Pentecostalism.* Darton, Longman, and Todd, 1976.

1910 Turner, George A. "The Baptism of the Holy Spirit in the Wesleyan Tradition," *WTJ* 14 (Spring 1979): 50–76.

1911 ______. "Doctrine of Sanctification," in *The Distinctive Emphasis of Asbury Theological Seminary,* Harold B. Kuhn, editor. Asbury Seminary, 1963. Pp. 78–100.

1912 ______. "The Holy Spirit in the Hermeneutics of the Reformation and the Radical Reformation," in *Essays on Apostolic Themes: Studies in Honor of Howard M. Ervin.* Paul Elbert, editor. Hendrickson Publishers, 1985. Pp. 15–22.

1913 ______. *The More Excellent Ways: The Scriptural Basis of the Wesleyan Message.* Light and Life Press, 1951.

1914 Turner, Max M. B. "Concept of Receiving the Spirit in John's Gospel," in *Vox Evangelica X,* Donald Guthrie, editor. Vox Evangelica, 1977. Pp. 24–42.

1915 ______. "Jesus and the Spirit in Lucan Perspective," *TB* 32 (1981): 3–42.

1916 ______. "The Significance of Receiving the Spirit in Luke–Acts: A Survey of Modern Scholarship," *TJ* ns 2 (Fall 1981): 131–58.

1917 ______. "The Significance of Spirit Endowment for Paul," *Ev* 9 (1975): 56–80.

1918 ______. "Spirit Endowment in Luke–Acts: Some Linguistic Considerations," in *Biblical and Historical Essays from LBC,* H. Rowdon, editor. N.p., 1981. Pp. 112–34.

1919 Tuttle, James Edward. "The Communicative Impact of Focused Worship." Unpublished dissertation, Drew University, 1982.

1920 Tuttle, Robert G. *The Partakers: Holy Spirit Power for Persevering Christians.* Abingdon Press, 1974.

1921 Tyerman, Luke. *The Life of John Wesley.* 8 vols. Epworth, 1931.

1922 Underwood, Bernard E. *The Gifts of the Spirit: Supernatural Equipment for Christian Service.* Advocate Press, 1967.

1923 Unger, Merrill F. *The Baptism and Gifts of the Holy Spirit.* Moody Press, 1974.

1924 ______. *The Baptizing Work of the Holy Spirit.* Dunham Publishing Company, 1962.

1925 ______. "The Significance of Pentecost," *BS* 122 (April-June 1965): 169–77.

1926 Unnik, W. C. van. "De Heilige Geest in het Nieuwe Testament," in *De Spiritu Sancto,* Kemick, 1964. Pp. 63–75.

1927 Vallings, James F. *The Holy Spirit of Promise: Some Functions of the Most Holy Spirit of God Doctrinally and Devotionally Considered and Applied.* Skeffington and Son, 1897.

1928 Van Dusen, Henry P. *Spirit, Son and Father: Christian Faith in the Light of the Holy Spirit.* Scribner's, 1958.

1929 ______. "Third Force in Christianity," *Life* 50 (June 9, 1958): 113–24.

1930 Vanhoye, Albert. "Esprit Eternel et Feu du Sacrifice en He 9:14," *Bib* 64:2 (1983): 263–74.

1931 Vaporis, Nomikos M. "Second Ecumenical Synod, Constantinople, AD 381." 1600th anniversary symposia, New York and Brookline, Massachusetts, 1981.

1932 Vaughan, C. R. *The Gifts of the Spirit.* Presbyterian Committee of Publication, 1894.

1933 Vaughan, Curry Ned, Jr. "Building a Community of Faith." Unpublished dissertation, Drew University, 1980.

1934 Veenhof, Jan. "De Inwoning van de Geest en het Nieuwe Leven," in *Charismatisch Nederland,* Fem Rutke, editor. J. H. Kok, 1977. Pp. 49–56.

1935 ______. *De parrakleet.* J. H. Kok, 1974.

1936 Verghese, Paul. *Die orthodoxe Kirche und der Heilige Geist.* Edel, 1966.

1937 Vergote, Antoine. "De Geest, kracht tot heil en geestelijke gezondheid," in *Leven uit de geest.* Hilversum, 1974. Pp. 180–89.

1938 Verhees, Jacques. "Die Bedeutung des Geistes Gottes im Leben des Menschen nach Augustinus frühester Pneumatologie (Bis 391)," *ZKC* 88:2 3 (1977): 161–89.

1939 Verhees, Jacques. *God in beweging: Ein onderzoek naar de pneumatologie van Augustinus.* H. Veenman, 1968.

1940 Verryn, T. D. "Historical Perspectives on the Emphasis on the Holy Spirit," in *The Spirit in Biblical Perspective,* W. S. Vorster, editor. University of South Africa, 1980. Pp. 1–18.

1941 Versteeg, John M. *Perpetuating Pentecost.* Clark & Colby, 1930.

1942 Vigano, Egidio. "El Carisma de don Bosco," *EsTe* 6 (January-June 1979): 293–346.

1943 Vignaux, Paul. "La Sanctification par l'esprit incree d'après Jean de ripa, 1 sen dist XIV–XV," in *Miscellanea Andre Combes,* Antonio Piolanti, et al., editors. Libreria Editrice Della Pontificia Universitá, 1967. 2:285–317.

1944 Villalón, José R. *Sacrements dans l'Esprit: Existence humaine et théologie Sacramentelle.* Beauchesne, 1977.

1945 Visher, Lukas, ed. *Spirit of God, Spirit of Christ: Ecumenical Reflections on the Filioque Controversy.* World Council of Churches, 1981.

1946 Vischer, Wilhelm. "L'Esprit Saint," *ETR* 50:2 (1975): 225–29.

1947 Vitry, Ermin. "Filled with the Spirit," *Wor* 28:7 (1954): 328–38.

1948 Vivier, Lincoln Morse. "Glossolalia in the New Testament," *JETS* 7 (Spring 1964): 53–58.

1949 Voegtle, Anton. "Paraklese und Eschatologie nach Röm 13:11–14." Discussion paper.

1950 Vogel, Heinrich. "Die Predigt als Gehörte Rede," *EvTh* 39 (March-April 1979): 88–100.

1951 Volz, Paul. *Der Geist Gottes und die verwandten Erscheinungen im Alten Testament und im anschliessenden Judentum.* Mohr, 1910.

1952 Vonier, Anscar. *L'Esprit et l'épouse.* Les Editions du Cerf, 1947.

1953 Vorbichler, Anton. "Wenn Bantu Christen werden: Religionswissenschaftliche und Missionspastorale Analyse," *ZMR* 62 (January 1978): 1–20.

1954 Vorster, W. S. *The Spirit in Biblical Perspective (Proceedings of the 4th Symposium, Institute for Theological Research, Pretoria, SA, 1980).* University of South Africa, 1980.

1955 Vriezen, T. C. "De Heilige Geest in het Oude Testament," in *De Spiritu Sancto.* Kemick, 1964. Pp. 7–39.

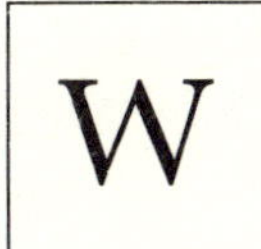

1956 Wackenheim, Charles. "Le christianisme, 'Religion du Salut,' " *RSciRel* 56 (October 1982): 274–84.

1957 Wainwright, A. W. *The Trinity in the New Testament.* SPCK, 1977.

1958 Wainwright, Geoffrey. "The Holy Spirit in the Life of the Church," *GOTR* 27 (Winter 1982): 441–53.

1959 Walker, Alan. *Breakthrough: Rediscovery of the Holy Spirit.* Abingdon Press, 1969.

1960 Walker, Anselm. "Sophiology," *Diak* 16:1 (1981): 40–54.

1961 Walker, James B. *The Doctrine of the Holy Spirit.* Griggs & Company, 1874.

1962 ______. *God's Wisdom in the Plan of Salvation.* Higley Press, 1958.

1963 Wallis, Jim. "Anointed by the Spirit," *JCQ* 43 (Fall 1977): 231–34.

1964 Wallis, Russell W. "The Holy Spirit as Related to the Person and Work of Christ." Unpublished dissertation, Southwestern Baptist Seminary, 1949.

1965 Walpole, George H. *The Mission of the Holy Ghost.* Longmans, Green and Co., 1908.

1966 Walter, Wilhelm. *Das Zeugnis des Heiligen Geistes nach Luther und nach moderner Schwärmerei.* Dörffling & Franke, 1899.

1967 Walton, Daniel. *The Witness of the Spirit.* Lane & Tippett, 1847.

1968 Walvoord, John F. "Contemporary Issues in the Doctrine of the Holy Spirit, Part IV: Spiritual Gifts Today," *BS* 130 (1973): 315–28.

1969 ______. *The Doctrine of the Holy Spirit: A Study in Pneumatology.* Dallas Theological Seminary, 1943.

1970 ______. *The Holy Spirit: A Comprehensive Study of the Person and Work of the Holy Spirit.* Dunham Publishing Company, 1958.

1971 ______. *The Holy Spirit at Work Today.* Moody Press, 1973.

1972 Ward, Wayne E. "The Significance of Tongues for the Church," in *Speaking in Tongues: Let's Talk About It,* Watson E. Mills, editor. Word Books, 1973. Pp. 143–51.

1973 Ware, Ann P. "Brief for Truly Ecumenical Worship," *ChrCent* 93 (April 21, 1976): 387–91.

1974 Warren, John Frank, III. "An Investigation of Children's Beliefs in Transcendent Figures." Unpublished dissertation, Duke University, 1980.

1975 Washburn, William I. *The Holy Spirit: A Layman's Conception.* G. P. Putnams, 1918.

1976 Watkin-Jones, Howard. *The Holy Spirit from Arminius to Wesley.* Epworth, 1928.

1977 ______. "The Holy Spirit in the Church," in *The Doctrine of the Holy Spirit,* Vincent Taylor, editor. Epworth, 1937. Pp. 69–104.

1978 ______. *The Holy Spirit in the Mediaeval Church.* Epworth, 1922.

1979 Watson, David C. K. *One in the Spirit.* Revell Co., 1973.

1980 Watson, G. D. *Types of the Holy Spirit.* Revivalist Office, n.d.

1981 Watson, Nigel M. "Risen Christ and Spirit/Paraclete in the Fourth Gospel," *ABR* 31 (October 1983): 81–85.

1982 Watson, Richard. *Life of Reverend John Wesley.* Carlton & Porter, 1831.

1983 ______. *Works.* John Mason, 1834.

1984 Watts, Gary Lynn. "The Theological Methods of G. C. Berkouwer." Unpublished dissertation, Fuller Theological Seminary, 1981.

1985 Weakley, Clare. *The Holy Spirit and Power.* Logos International, 1977.

1986 Webb, Allan B. *The Presence and Office of the Holy Spirit.* W. Skeffington & Son, 1881.

1987 Webb, Douglas. "La doctrine du Saint-Esprit dans le liturgie eucharistique d'après les théologiens anglais des 17 et 18 siècles," in *Le Saint-Esprit dans la Liturgie,* A. Pistoia and A. Triacca, editors. Bibliotheca Ephemerides Liturgicae, 1977. Pp. 165–81.

1988 Weborg, C. John. "Study of Schleiermacher's Concept of Faith," *CQ* 36 (Fall 1978): 39–48.

1989 Weinel, Heinrich. *Die Wirkungen des Geistes und Geister im nachapostolischen Zeitalter bis auf Irenäus.* Mohr, 1899.

1990 Weinrich, W. C. *Spirit and Martyrdom: A Study of Work of the Holy Spirit in Contexts of Persecution and Martyrdom in the New Testament and Early Christian Literature.* University Press of America, 1981.

1991 Weisiger, Cary Nelson, III. "The Doctrine of the Holy Spirit in the Preaching of Richard Sibbes." Unpublished dissertation, Fuller Theological Seminary, 1984.

1992 Weitbrecht, H. J. "Ekstatische Zunstände bei Schizophrenen," in *Beitrage zur Ekstase,* T. Spörri, editor. S. Karger, 1968. Pp. 232–45.

1993 Welliver, Kenneth Bruce. "Pentecost and the Early Church." Unpublished dissertation, Yale University, 1961.

1994 Wendbourg, Dorothea. "From the Cappadocian Fathers to Gregory Palamas: The Defeat of Trinitarian Theology," in *Studia Patristica,* E. Livingstone, editor. 1982. Vol. 17, pt. 1.

1995 Wendelborn, Gert. "Luther und Muentzer," *CV* 18:1 (1975): 57–75.

1996 Wendland, Heinz D. "Das Wirken des Heiligen Geistes in den Glaübigen nach Paulus," in *Pro Veritate, ein Theologischer Dialog: L. Jaeger,* Edmund Schlink, editor. Ascheddorffsche Verlagsbuchhandlung, 1963. Pp. 133–56.

1997 Wenger, J. C. "The Anabaptist Perspective on the Holy Spirit," in *Encounter with the Holy Spirit,* George R. Brunk, II, editor. Herald Press, 1972. Pp. 81–100.

1998 Wesley, Charles. *Journal.* R. Culley, 1910.

1999 Wesley, John. *The Holy Spirit and Power.* Logos International, 1977.

2000 Wessels, Roland Heinrich. "The Doctrine of the Baptism in the Holy Spirit Among the Assemblies of God." Unpublished dissertation, Pacific School of Religion, 1966.

2001 Westall, M. R. "Scope of the Term 'Spirit of God' in the Old Testament," *IJT* 26 (January-March 1977): 29–43.

2002 Westgarth, J. W. *The Holy Spirit and the Primitive Mind.* Victory Press, 1946.

2003 Wetter, Friedrich. "Amor Mutuus und Amor Reflexus: Überlegungen zu Hervorgang des Heiligen Geistes," in *Wahrheit und Verkündikung: M. Schmaus,* Leo Scheffczyk, et al., editors. Verlag Ferdinand Schöningh, 1967. Pp. 701–31.

2004 Whalley, W. E. "Pentecostal Theology," *BQ* 27 (July 1978): 282–89.

2005 Wheeler, Paul. "The Pauline Development of the Doctrine of the Holy Spirit." Unpublished dissertation, Southern Baptist Seminary, 1924.

2006 Wheelock, Donald Ray. "Spirit Baptism in American Pentecostal Thought." Unpublished dissertation, Emory University, 1983.

2007 Whitcomb, John C. "Contemporary Apologetics and the Christian Faith," *BS* 134 (April-June 1977): 99–106.

2008 White, Barrie Leroy. "An Educational Approach to Developing Healthy Self-Esteem in Christian Individuals." Unpublished dissertation, Eastern Baptist Seminary, 1981.

2009 White, Reginald E. O. *The Answer Is the Spirit.* Westminster Press, 1979.

2010 Whitehead, John. *The Life of the Reverend John Wesley.* 2 vols. Stephen Conchman, 1793.

2011 Widmann, Martin. "1 Kor 2:6–16: Ein Einspruch gegen Paulus," *ZNW* 70:1–2 (1979): 44–53.

2012 Wierwille, Victor Paul. *Receiving the Holy Spirit Today.* The Way, 1957.

2013 Wilcox, Leslie D. *Be Ye Holy: A Study of the Teachings of Scripture Relative to Entire Sanctification with a Sketch of the History and the Literature of the Holiness Movement.* The Revivalist Press, 1965.

2014 Wild, Robert. " 'It Is Clear That There Are Serious Differences Among You' (1 Corinthians 1:11): The Charismatic Renewal Entering Religious Communities," *RevRel* 32 (September 1973): 1093–1102.

2015 ______. "The Post-Charismatic Phenomena: A Theological Interpretation," *RevRel* 41 (March-April 1982): 257–65.

2016 Wiles, Maurice F. "The Holy Spirit and the Incarnation," in *The Holy Spirit,* Dow Kirkpatrick, editor. Tidings, 1974. Pp. 90–104.

2017 Wilkens, Wilhelm. "Kirche, Geist, und Taufe im Neuen Testament," in *Warum Christen Ihre Kinder: H. Gollwitzer,* D. Schellong, editor. N.p., 1969. 112–45.

2018 ______. "Wassertaufe und Geistesempfang bei Lukas," *ThZ* 23 (1967): 26–47.

2019 Willebrands, Jan G. M. Cardinal. "Le Dialogue entre Catholiques et Anglicans (Lecture at Anglican-Roman Catholic Symposium, Toronto, 1979)," *Iren* 52:3 (1979): 323–43.

2020 ______. "Le Concile de Constantinople de 381, 2E Ecumenique: Son Importance et Son Actualité," *Iren* 54:2 (1981): 163–91.

2021 Williams, Charles. *The Descent of the Dove.* Longmans, Green & Co., 1939.

2022 Williams, Colin W. *Our Power: The Holy Spirit.* Methodist Publishing House, n.d.

2023 Williams, J. Rodman. *The Era of the Spirit.* Logos International, 1971.

2024 ______. "The Gift of the Holy Spirit Today," *JETS* 26 (December 1983): 472–73.

2025 ______. "The Holy Spirit and Eschatology," *P* 3:2 (Fall 1981): 54–58.

2026 ______. "Opinion," *LJ* 7:3 (May-June 1977): 35.

2027 ______. "Pentecostal Theology: A Neo-Pentecostal Viewpoint," in *Perspectives on the New Pentecostalism,* Russell P. Spittler, editor. Baker Book House, 1976. Pp. 111–32.

2028 ______. "Profile of the Charismatic Movement," *CT* 19 (February 28, 1975): 9–13.

2029 ______. "The Upsurge of Pentecostalism: Some Presbyterian/Reformed Comment," *RefW* 31 (1971): 339–48.

2030 Williams, John. *The Holy Spirit, Lord and Life-Giver: A Biblical Introduction to the Doctrine of the Holy Spirit.* Loizeaux Brothers, 1980.

2031 Williams, Melvin D. *Community in a Black Pentecostal Church: An Anthropological Study.* University of Pittsburgh Press, 1974.

2032 ______. "Considerations of a Black Anthropologist Researching Pentecostalism," *Sp* 3:2 (1979): 20–26.

2033 Williams, Rowan. "Wort und Geist," in *Das religiöse Bewusstsein und der Heilige Geist in der Kirche,* Klaus Kremkau, editor. Otto Lembeck, 1980. Pp. 77–94.

2034 Wilmore, Gayraud S. and James H. Cone, eds. *Black Theology: A Documentary History, 1966–1979.* Orbis Books, 1979.

2035 Wilson, Emmanuel Munda. "Toward a Mende Christian Theology (Sierra Leone)." Unpublished dissertation, Fuller Theological Seminary, School of World Mission, 1982.

2036 Wilson, Karl K. "The Work of the Holy Spirit in Regeneration." Unpublished master's thesis, Princeton Theological Seminary, 1943.

2037 Windisch, Hans, with James W. Cox (trans.). *The Spirit-Paraclete in the Fourth Gospel.* Fortress Press, 1968.

2038 Winget, Wilfred Lamont. "The Holy Spirit and the Holiness of the Church: A Study in the Theology of the Church of the Nazarene." Unpublished dissertation, Vanderbilt University, 1966.

2039 Winkler, Gabriele. "A Remarkable Shift in the 4th Century Creeds: An Analysis of the Armenian, Syriac and Greek Evidence," in *Studia Patristica,* E. Livingstone, editor. 1982. Vol. 17, pt. 3.

2040 Winn, Albert C. "Holy Spirit and the Christian Life," *Int* 33 (January 1979): 47–57.

2041 ______. *The Inquirer Directed to an Experimental and Practical View of the Work of the Holy Spirit.* Robert Carter & Brothers, 1840.

2042 Winslow, Octavius. *The Work of the Holy Spirit.* Banner of Truth Trust, 1972.

2043 Winstanley, E. W. *Spirit in the New Testament.* Cambridge University Press, 1908.

2044 Winstone, Harold. *Pastoral Liturgy: A Symposium.* Collins, 1975.

2045 Winward, Stephen F. *Fruit of the Spirit.* InterVarsity Press, 1981.

2046 Wirt, Sherwood E. *Freshness of the Spirit.* Harper and Row, 1978.

2047 Wisloff, Fredrik, with Ingvald Daehlin (trans.). *I Believe in the Holy Spirit.* Augsburg Publishing Co., 1949.

2048 Wogen, Norris L. *Jesus, Where Are You Taking Us: Messages from the First International Lutheran Conference on the Holy Spirit.* Creation House, 1973.

2049 Wolff, Salin-Mary. "Question in the Theology of the Religious Life: Sainte Madeleine Sophie Barat on Prayer," *ETL* 50 (December 1974): 284–313.

2050 Wolfram, Walter Andrew. "The Sociolinguistics of Glossolalia." Unpublished master's thesis, Hartford Seminary, 1966.

2051 Womack, David A. *The Wellsprings of the Pentecostal Movement.* Gospel Publishing House, 1968.

2052 Wood, Arthur K. *The Burning Heart: John Wesley, Evangelist.* Eerdmans Publishing Co., 1967.

2053 Wood, Arthur S. *The Inextinguishable Blaze.* Eerdmans Publishing Co., 1968.

2054 ______. *Paul's Pentecost: Studies in the Life of the Spirit from Romans 8.* Paternoster Press, 1963.

2055 Wood, Charles M. "Aim of Christian Theology," *PJ* 31 (Spring 1978): 22–29.

2056 Wood, Irving F. *The Spirit of God in Biblical Literature.* A. C. Armstrong & Son, 1904.

2057 Wood, J. A. *Perfect Love, or . . . Christian Holiness.* The Christian Witness Company, 1910.

2058 Wood, Laurence W. "Exegetical-Theological Reflections on the Baptism with the Holy Spirit," *WTJ* 14 (Fall 1979): 51–63.

2059 Wood, William W. "Culture and Personality Aspects of the Pentecostal Holiness Religion." Unpublished dissertation, University of North Carolina, 1961.

2060 Woodhouse, H. F., et al., eds. *Directions: Theology in a Changing Church.* SPCK, 1970.

2061 ______. "How the Life Giver Acts in History," *MC* ns 21:4 (1978): 32–35.

2062 ______. "The Holy Spirit, the Authority of the Church and Development in Doctrine," in *Directions: Theology in a Changing Church,* H. Woodhouse, et al., editors. SPCK, 1970. Pp. 45–61.

2063 "The Work of the Holy Spirit," in *Church Studies on the Holy Spirit,* Marvin Simmers, editor. John Knox Press, 1983. Pp. 30–69.

2064 World Alliance of Reformed Churches. Baptist World Alliance. "Holy Spirit: Baptism, Membership in the Church of Christ," *RefW* 35 (September 1978): 114–19.

2065 Worsfold, J. E. "A Theology of the Holy Spirit," in *Religious Studies in the Pacific,* J. Hinchcliff, editor. Tidings Publishing Co., 1978. Pp. 12–24.

2066 Wright, Charles D. "The Three Temptations and the Seven Gifts of the Holy Spirit in 'Guthlac A,' " *Tra* 38 (1982): 341–43.

2067 Wright, John H. "Authority in the Church Today: A Theological Reflection," *Com* 7 (Winter 1980): 364–82.

2068 ______. "Meaning and Structure of Catholic Faith," *ThSt* 39 (December 1978): 701–18.

2069 Wright, Walter C. "The Source of Paul's Concept of Pneuma," *CQ* 41 (February 1983): 17–26.

2070 Wunderlick, Lorenz. *The Half-Known God: The Lord and Giver of God.* Concordia Publishing House, 1963.

2071 Wynkoop, Mildred Bangs. "The Communion of the Holy Spirit." Unpublished essay, n.d.

2072 ______. *Foundations of Wesleyan-Arminian Theology.* Beacon Hill Press, 1967.

2073 ______. *John Wesley: Revolutionary.* Beacon Hill Press, 1970.

2074 ______. "Theological Roots of Wesleyanism's Understanding of the Holy Spirit," *WTJ* 14 (Spring 1979): 77–98.

Y

2075 Yaghjian, Lucretia B. "Hermetic Art, or the Holy Spirit and Us: Narrative Sense or Secrecy in the Hermeneutic of Frank Kermode," *CL* 30:1 (Fall 1980): 64–79.

2076 Yanovsky, V. S., et al., eds. *The Third Hour: In Memory of Helen Iswolsky.* The Third Hour Foundation, 1976.

2077 Yates, John E. *The Spirit and the Kingdom.* N.p., 1963.

2078 Yerkes, James O. " 'Glauben und Genuss': Hegel, Luther, and the Holy Spirit," *CSR* 12:3 (1983): 237–43.

2079 Yim, Howard R. "Preaching God's Word 'in Demonstration of the Spirit and Power,' " in *Essays on Apostolic Themes: Studies in Honor of Howard M. Ervin.* Paul Elbert, editor. Hendrickson Publishers, 1985. Pp. 71–81.

2080 Yi, Richard. "Spirit Baptism and Tongues in Acts." Unpublished thesis, Talbot Theological Seminary, 1969.

2081 Yoder, J. Otis. "The Prophetic Work of the Spirit," in *Encounter with the Holy Spirit,* George R. Brunk, II, editor. Herald Press, 1972. Pp. 136–55.

2082 Young, John Terry. "The Holy Spirit and the Birth of Churches," in *The Birth of Churches: A Biblical Basis,* Talmadge R. Amberson, editor. Broadman Press, 1979. Pp. 163–79.

2083 ______. *The Spirit Within You.* Broadman Press, 1977.

2084 Young, Sherman Plato. "The Doctrine of the Holy Spirit in Relation to Methodist Theology: An Historical Survey and Constructive Statement in the Light of Modern Philosophical and Psychological Trends." Unpublished dissertation, Drew University, 1930.

Z

2085 Zartmann, Rufus C. *The Holy Spirit.* Central Publishing House, 1930.

2086 Zaugg, Elmer A. *A Genetic Study of the Spirit Phenomena in the New Testament.* University of Chicago Press, 1917.

2087 Zehr, Paul M. "The Gifts of the Spirit," in *Encounter with the Holy Spirit,* George R. Brunk, II, editor. Herald Press, 1972. Pp. 46–62.

2088 Zens, Jon. "An Appraisal of the Charismatic Movement," *BRR* 11:2 (1982): 43–47.

2089 Ziener, Georg. "Der Heilige Geist und die Anfänge der Kirche (1 Cor 12, 13, 14)," in *Miscellanea Fuldensia: Adolf Bolte,* Franz Scholz, editor. Parzeller, 1966. Pp. 97–108.

2090 Zimany, Roland D. "Enduring Values of Luther's Approach to Knowing God," *LQ* 27 (February 1975): 6–26.

2091 Zimmerman, Charles. "Priorities and Beliefs of Pentecostals," *CT* 25 (September 4, 1981): 36–67.

2092 Zimmerman, Thomas F. "Plea for the Pentecostalists," *CT* 7 (January 4, 1963): 11–12.

2093 ______. "The Pentecostal Position," *PE* (February 10, 1963): 2–3, 7.

2094 ______. "The Reason for the Rise of the Pentecostal Movement," in *Aspects of Pentecostal-Charismatic Origins,* Vinson Synan, editor. Logos International, 1975. Pp. 5–13.

2095 ______. "Where Is the 'Third Force' Going?" *CT* 4 (August 1, 1960): 15–16, 18.

2096 Zuck, Roy B. *The Holy Spirit in Your Teaching.* Victor Books, 1984.

2097 ______. "The Place of the Holy Spirit in Christian Education." Unpublished dissertation, Dallas Theological Seminary, 1961.

2098 Zylberberg, Jacques and Jean Montminy. "Reproduction socio-politique et Production symbolique: engagement et désengagement des charismatiques catholiques québécois," *ARSSR* 4 (1980): 121–48.

INDEXES

Scripture References

Subjects